Adventures in New Lands: Volume 5

Other titles in this series

Volume 1: *Inuit Folk-tales* by Knud Rasmussen
Volume 2: *Journal in Greenland* by Hans Egede
Volume 3: *Vikings of Today* by Wilfred Grenfell
Volume 4: *Tales of Yukaghir* by Waldemar Bogoras

Eden of the North

Signe Rink

Translated by
L.S. Johanson

Originally published as
Koloni-Idyller fra Grønland,
Copenhagen, 1888

First English edition
copyright 2014 IPI Press

Design: IPI Press

ISBN 978-0-9829155-6-1

✦

International Polar Institute Press
Post Office Box 212
Hanover, New Hampshire 03755 USA

Eden of the North

by
Signe Rink

Translated by L.S. Johanson

Distributed by University Press of New England
upne.com

Translator's Note

These stories trace Signe Rink's intimate experiences growing up in Greenland using her own unique language.

The vast and powerful land and seascapes present a world of complexity that on occasion transcend language altogether. Translating this sense of place and wonder amid the natural world from Danish to English is challenging for both the eye and ear.

In describing domestic life in nineteenth century Colonial Greenland, a quiet simplicity is present honoring simple tasks and scarce resources—necessities, rather than any agenda, religious or political.

Rink's tender capacity for touching the mythical and dream-like worlds beyond the realities of Greenlandic and Colonial daily life calls for a poetic crafting of language that can occasionally, in its gentle strangeness, transport us to memories of our own experiences.

To convey the world of Signe Rink's writing faithfully, this translation attempts to provide the reader with a contextual fabric that balances each of these historical, geographical and cultural elements.

L. Johanson

Contents

Map of locations mentioned in this text   13

The Two Elses   15
Teisten   125

Biographical note   158

1. *Sisemiut*
2. *Qaqartoq*
3. *Mt. Malene (Little Malene)*
4. *Qaanaaq*
5. *Tingmissat (proximate)*
6. *Land of the Innersuit*
7. *Nuuk, capital of Greenland*
8. *Baffin Bay*

13

The Two Elses

✦

Our Colony is named after the Greenlandic word for "nose" or spit, and the houses are scattered across the little valley floor banked by a higher plateau that reaches down to the sea. At the height of land one can see, in descending order, first the church spire and its cross standing highest above the village, followed by the parish minister's house, then the houses belonging to the Chief Inspector, the Doctor, and the Colonial Magistrate. Further down there is the

The Two Elses

schoolhouse, and then the weather-beaten, stone cottages built with more integrity than their neighboring modern buildings, one of which is two storied.

Between these buildings spread across both sides of the wide road which splits the Colony in half are the houses built by the Greenlanders, some with peaked rooflines, others flat. These native-built cottages are especially beautiful when the green grass finally takes hold, almost completely covering the stonework that can be seen in walls between layers of grass turf and mortar.

Often you can see the goats brought over by the Danes standing and nipping a fresh little meal from these sap green walls. A few of the cottage huts seem broken down and neglected, as if they had dried up altogether, especially those with flat roofs, for they were covered by strangely colored sheathing once used to build kayaks that only the women use. Yet even the poorest of these cottages lends color to the painted landscape of our Colony as they lie sprinkled here and there, tucked into the steep hillsides and along the village footpaths . . . at least when viewed from a distance.

To the south and north, the colony is surrounded by two heather crested arms wrapping around in a curved embrace towards the sea. It is almost as if there is a little hesitation in the embrace, as one arm suddenly pulls back, doubting, and stopping right in front of the "Flagpole Hill" while the opposite arm reaches out further, suddenly decisive enough to push out the spit we call "Fat House Nose," which then creates a harbor for small boats.

Harbor seal hunters bring their blubber catch here to be weighed and this is also where the blubber is boiled down to oil at the rendering plant. Seal blubber is rendered into vats and stored for the summer season when big ships pick it up.

Old boats are also moored and in dry dock at the rendering plant harbor, where lumber is stacked for boat building and stored in a small shipyard. Children in the colony usually love to play here, but today they seem to be busy elsewhere. Only the ring of the carpenter's hammer tells us that anyone is out on the "Fat House Nose."

In front of one of the houses, two elderly unmarried women are sitting in a clean swept spot sorting down feathers. One woman is bowed over on an old chair with a very tired leather seat stuffed with hay, more hay than leather, while the second woman is sitting atop an old wooden bucket ringed with iron bands. The heavy down carder, or "harp," as it is called, lies across both their laps, and at each side rests a couple sacks of feathers, holding the clean and unsorted down respectively. With their right, then with the left hand, each woman rolls the down across the seal

The Two Elses

hide strings of the Kobbe-Rem[1] harp as little twigs, leaves and debris fall between the strings, gathering in piles below.

A pretty young wife sits on a rock fallen from the stone house walls. She has a pale blue ribbon wrapped around her hair. She is watching a little boy who runs around with bow and arrow. On the rocky shore above the high water-mark, the boy's father is repairing his kayak. His fishing gear lies all around him, spread out, and he is deep in thought, concentrating on his work.

The old women are turning handfuls of feathers into their harp-carder, removing clean batches and examining them in the sunlight to make sure every last piece of twig, leaf, straw and feather pin—the last reminder of the bird and her soft nest plundered for feathers—is plucked carefully out meticulously by hand and laid to rest in the clean pile of down.

In the warm sunlight the pile of soft down rises like a great gray wave swelling upwards from the carpet of the earth. The old women have no idea what kind of value such riches their down harvest would fetch on the other side of the sea.

Maren and the the somewhat younger Johanne-Marie work for the Colony Administration—we call it the Business Office—and the assistant manager, sometimes with the Magistrate himself, stops by to offer encouragement to the two old ladies, mentioning a little extra payment in coffee or tobacco for quick work. When cleaning down, fair weather makes all the difference.

The sun is too bright for old Maren, so she pulls down her headscarf to shade her red-rimmed eyes, sighing her customary, *Ah issikasika*! Oh, my old, tired eyes!" The old women chat softly about times gone by when things were better than the present . . . as old women often do, be they in silken blouses or sealskin leggings. They chat about times past on their many kayak adventures and long trips gathering eider down, about the days when arriving ships were greeted with canon blasts from Flagpole Hill and when a docking ship would not stay in port for days or weeks, but rather months, and how the young folk would be allowed everywhere below decks, when now nobody was even allowed above deck! And the wonderful Greenlandic dances, when dear old "Mammalak" [2] presided. Mammalak, who had long since stepped down, and who had married a native girl—in short, the kind of good

---

1. *Kobbe-Rem is the name of the strong rope made from thin strips of the hide of the harbor seal, a vital product for the local Greenlandic economy.*
2. *The colonial Magistrate was nicknamed Mammalak for his gourmet tastes, and his favorite phrase in Greenlandic meaning, "delicious."*

The Two Elses

old days when everything seemed so much more open and easy . . .

The Colony lies sheltered and warmed by the sun between steep hills, while the stone giants of the inland mountains tower above the village like massive, immobile silent spectators watching every little human change in the valley floor . . . towering above everything, with their icy peaked caps above brown fields or white snow, summer and winter. Now it is summer and the purple heather blooms on every hill top, and the Colony children, those who have not run out to play far away, are playing "kitchen" and "house" in the hills.

Outside the cottages a single Greenlandic woman is squatting in the warm sun, while another is bowed over the *Kamiutstick*, a flat piece of wood about three feet in length bound with iron at the end. It is used for softening leather leggings and footwear by pulling rawhides back and forth over its tip. There is no breeze today; everything is bathed in sunlight, bringing out the mosquito swarms from damp grassy spots in the Danish potato patches behind red painted fences. Windows are closed against the mosquitoes today . . . perhaps also because the Danes have left to trek up into the hills, everyone except for the Magistrate and the Minister's wife—the minister himself being away on business matters.

The unusual sleepy calm of this warm afternoon might also be attributed to the fact that many young native villagers went along as porters to guide, carry and help the Danes on their day long Highland walking adventure, leaving the village relatively unpopulated for a few hours. Yet, the warm, sleepy haze seems to slip out across the sea, settling over a few fishermen in their kayaks, who hardly appear to have moved at all for hours, looking like tiny black dots far away, melting into a black smear on the horizon of the sea. Only the ring of the carpenter's hammer breaks the silence down at the boatyard behind the "Fat House Nose," not really erasing the silence, but increasing it by remarkable contrast.

The old women are piling batches of eider down feathers onto the growing mountain of white sitting upon the cloth. Amalie, the younger wife with the blue ribbon is enjoying the sight of her little boy chasing small birds, which so far seem to be able to escape his attacks. Amalie, who has considerable girth, rises up periodically, growing ever more excited, rocking back and forth from heel to toe and crying out "Ta, ta, ta look at that now . . ." whispering and gesturing to the older ladies looking down over to her little boy, Epha. They look up when they hear the sound of a "twang!"—and see an arrow flying through the air and the boy with his bow.

The Two Elses

An exclamation of "oohhh!" resounds as a little robin lays wounded on the ground from a shot to the wing.

The mother, Amalie, rushes to her son and begins shouting down to her husband who was working his kayak. With great pride, she calls, "Steffan, Steffan! Come and see what Epha hit." The father's face lights up as he calls back, "Ja, of course, now who would be surprised about that?" Grandmother Johanne-Marie rains down her praise over the promising grandson. A man's voice from the road shouts, "Come Johanne-Marie, the Pastor's wife needs you now!"

Johanne-Marie drops the down harp immediately, as does old Maren who was also called upon at precisely the very same moment, albeit from one of the Greenlandic houses from the other side of the road.[3] These elders are elevated in their status in the village; Johanne-Marie had been educated during a stay in Denmark with the aforementioned Magistrates family which gave her some feeling of pride in her situation—and old Maren had achieved her position of power through empirical trials in the land[4] itself. Johanne-Marie primarily saw her loyalties as lying with the Danes and the pending needs of the Danish Minister's wife, so she bowed and disappeared into the entryway of the house belonging to her son-in-law, Steffan Egedes, the house in front of which the two old women had sat picking eider down feathers in the warm afternoon light. Meanwhile, Maren, with no further ado, dashes across the road to the Greenlander house from which the call came in need of her to appear.

But what of the down harp and the piece work; the reward and promise of coffee and tobacco offered by the Magistrate himself? Well, it must be Amalie's lot to take care of that unfinished business. She quickly wraps up the clean pile in the cloth and rests the bundle against the wall of the house. Then she carries the remaining eider down and all its bits of straw, leaves, twigs and debris that had not been removed up into the loft, the extra room above formed in cottages by their peaked roofs, as opposed to those dwellings which had only flat ones.

No other ladder led up to this loft other than the stones sticking out from the unplastered walls and turf patches clinging to the sides of the house. Amalie balances and climbs up in zigzag fashion with great care to reach the little entry door to the loft. She could jump down in one leap when she needs to get down, since these humble Greenlandic dwellings were not very

---

3. *The road is significant in that it is paved and it literally divides the Colony in half.*
4. *Greenland is sometimes referred to, in short, by her natives as "the land."*

The Two Elses

high off the ground. But she forgot to set the latch of a stick across the little door and so she had to make another trip up to secure her goods—this rather trusting custom was considered all that was needed to lock up one's home in the village.

That morning the Danish Minister's little wife had woken up with a sudden desire to do something, and so every task imaginable had been taken up with enthusiastic gusto.

First, all the wine which had recently arrived with the last summer ship, the very ship which had unloaded and was now preparing to set sail out of the harbor, was to be unpacked and stored properly in the Parish cellar, including the reds, the whites and the port, as well as the altar wine, even if Cook needed extra help to get it done. Then all the flowers had to be removed from the window boxes and shelves inside the house, all flowerpots cleaned and sorted, and all dead leaves, petals and stems removed, which in fact only existed in the imagination of her ladyship. She then took up battle with the lovely billowing clouds of lacy lobelias which could not have been more beautiful at that moment, energetically destroying them by tearing the blooms into units of order to be tied into lines decorating the walls and other places where they were not growing. Her next point of attack was the guest room, which certainly needed to be aired out, along with the minister's private study, where books needed a firm dusting especially by her very own hand. And so it went all day; she threw herself into everything and it was all done thoroughly and with conviction.

Now, she thought, it should be wonderful to rest after a full day's work, especially since everyone had gone away to the Highland trekking tour, leaving her in peace to contemplate the absence of her husband. What might he be thinking, was he thinking of her? Was he looking forward to his return and to seeing her again? As much as she was looking forward to seeing him again? They had never been apart from each other for this amount of time!

She had no idea why she was suddenly starting to cry when she felt so immeasurably happy and content! It must be because she was just tired, she had taken on so much today, and she simply needed to learn how to pace herself.

She gazed out over her sweet smelling, fragrant flower boxes and allowed her eyes to wander across the rooflines of her Colony—the Parish House stands above all the others on the hillside, allowing for excellent views of everything below—and her eyes follow the horizon across the sea where fishing kayaks bob gently, and her gaze continues past the islands in the west. Her thoughts had run their course, and she fell into a partially sad but slightly sweet melancholy day dream. Suddenly, a strange and unusual desire to see Johanne- Marie broke into

The Two Elses

her reverie. She calls sharply and Johanne-Marie appears, reluctantly, which might have been calculated to garner confidence as she preferred not to appear too eager. The little Parish wife took her by both hands, generating a surprised sound from Johanne-Marie who was led into the bedroom where a sight unfolded before her very eyes. The room was in a great state of disorder—drawers pulled out, and piles of children's' clothing were heaped everywhere—enough to clothe at least twenty Greenlandic children, but these children are somewhat small and require far less than other children do.

"God always helps those in need, isn't it true Johanne?" she asks pitifully.

Johanne answers, if somewhat gruffly, "*Sorungna*. Of course, but don't you think I helped plenty too, including many Danes as well ..."

"If only the pastor was home now, Johanne."

"*Sussasok*, and what would that help? Who needs a fifth wheel for their wagon?"

Johanne-Marie understood enough practical Danish to get by when it came to daily tasks, but she never offered anything when it came to speaking the language. Her pride was the cause, for she had never allowed a single Danish word to cross her lips even during her stay in Denmark. She had not, however, been able to refuse the hand of marriage to her Danish husband, but the "Cooper," as he was known, had long since passed away, leaving her a widow.

Johanne-Marie commanded a great deal of respect, the kind offered freely to those unique individuals who may not necessarily be charming, popular or easy, but trustworthy she was, you could always count on her steadiness.

A messenger arrives wanting to know if she desired payment in coffee or snuff tobacco for the eider down she had processed that day. She sends him off with an irritable reply, as this was not the best moment for market negotiations.

Old Maren, on the other hand, knew exactly what she wanted when questioned, and could not comprehend why anyone would ever be in doubt as to which was the better deal.

Of course, she understood how problematic it might be if your patient was Danish, "that was a different matter entirely," she voiced, with some sharpness.

The majestic Johanne-Marie sits in silence beside the Pastor's wife daydreaming about how it could be that the world's first mother had given birth to Cain.

"What are you thinking about Johanne-Marie?" sighs the little Pastor's wife, whose thoughts still circle around her husband's hopefully impending arrival.

Johanne-Marie keeps her own counsel and her reply redirects the conversation towards the arrival of an entirely different expected guest. She exclaims in Greenlandic, "*Uvatsie*! Have pa-

The Two Elses

tience, he will be here soon, but it takes time . . ." However, even the wisest of the old women in the village do not know everything, and before Johanne-Marie could take up the stray threads of her musings on Cain and Abel, the Pastor's soft cradle had tipped out its contents. The happy sounds of the little pastor's daughter erupted into their quiet space. As the good news of the arrival of a little girl spreads, well-wishers begin to arrive, returning with the Colony Magistrate and the Pastor himself, who was promoted to a higher post that night, somewhere further north.

Steffan was quite convinced that details would soon follow regarding their new home, to which the Colony Magistrate responded in Greenlandic, "*Taimaisassimavunga*! Peace and quiet, day and night, is what you can expect, where you are headed," which was exactly what Steffan was secretly hoping for.

An hour later the new mother opened her eyes following her first refreshing nap of the blessed. She was rather surprised, since she was inexperienced in the ways of native Greenlandic culture, to find she was alone in her room with a man dressed from head to toe in skins. He now stood staring at her openly from the end of her bed with a look of gentle awe. The crimson shade that began to spread across the patient's pale cheeks was soon correctly interpreted, together with the silent question forming on her lips, by the Cook Daniel. He fathomed that she wanted to know why Johanne-Marie had gone from the sick room. His answer came, surprisingly, in perfect Danish, "Oh I was just going to tell you—my wife has just given birth to a little girl—I asked for Johanne-Marie to go down to her. I will take damn good care of you meanwhile!" (It has become a custom for Danish speaking Greenlanders to throw in as many "damns" as possible, to make up for their lack of Danish vocabulary.)

The good Daniel Lunde, or Daniel the Cook as he was usually called, had a pair of rough, calloused hands capable of carrying coals or scratching up ice, but when he picked up a baby they were as soft as they could be. Seeing the way the baby was resting in her mothers arms, he bent over and shifted her around, apologizing to the young mother,

"You are not used to this kind of thing, you know, so I'll give you a little hand now."

He had finished everything in the kitchen, he explained, the oat gruel was already strained, the tea kettle simmered nicely, as it had been all night to comfort both his own wife in childbirth as well as the Pastor's wife during her labor, equally.

"Equally?" The Pastor's wife asked.

"Well, to be sure, not exactly equally," he had to admit.

The Two Elses

As a pastor's wife, the Danish lady enjoys comfort on every level and is surrounded by a lifestyle of luxury from top to toe. The Inuit mother, on the other hand, sits on old worn pillows, toughened by lean times, rocking her little brown baby to sleep in her arms. In a few days she will bind it to her back as she goes back to her daily chores, whether she or her baby need extra rest or not.

So the peaceful summer night stretches over the Colonial village. Only the whispers of elves playing with craggy ice-capped mountain giants can be heard as the shadows of the night steal the last kiss of sunlight.

The two births in the same hour—that became the favorite topic of the day—and everyone managed somehow to relate the story to their own lives or eventually turn their musings back to themselves one way or the other . . ." of course, it had to happen on the very day we go walking in the hills, and I never go up in those hills . . . ," Mrs. Buck, the Magistrate's wife was heard blustering. The other ladies were happily relieved that the long expectancy time was finally over, it would now be so much easier to offer up some helpful generosity to the new mother, their friend in the Parish House. Even children playing in the meadows argued over *who* saw the messengers first running to get the two old women to help out with the delivery. One of the children was even so bold as to speculate that it was "mysterious" that the two girls had arrived right when she was putting her eiderdown bird eggs into the cook pot.

Old Maren was complementing Daniel the Cook about the joys of his newly won fatherhood, fortuitously compounded by the coincidence of the double birthday to be shared with the pastor's daughter. Word travelled quickly throughout the Greenlandic cottages that it would be best if both girls were given the same name.[5]

The Greenlanders held sway and the girls were given the same name; as soon as the Pastor decided they would name their daughter Else, the Cook decided his daughter would have the same, with an added Greenlandic diminutive {rak} suffix of endearment, thus she became El'es'e and sometimes El'eseˆrak.

---

5. *Sharing a common birthday in Greenland, as well as sharing the given birth name, was considered an excuse for exchanging gifts, a custom which does not raise many issues when both parties are from the same country. When the persons invovled are from differing cultures, the Greenland native usually benefits greatly when the other party is Danish born. The Dane is obliged to offer little gifts to those Greenlanders whose names and birthdays are shared in common, though expectations from the Greenlander's side are usually humble and unspoken.*

The Two Elses

That the girls were to be christened on the same day was obvious to everyone.

At nine in the morning Daniel's wife arrived dressed in her best, holding her baby girl in a large white eider down quilt. In a shy gesture so characteristic of her Greenlandic culture, the mother's eyes furtively sought her own feet to make sure she was not dirtying the white floors of the Parish House. But she could not see below the billowing folds of the great white quilt which wrapped around her baby.

The Pastor's wife waved her forwards in a warm welcoming way and lifted a corner of the blanket to get a better look at the child. The baby was wide awake, looking straight into her eyes with that direct gaze only newborn babies are capable of. Maren understood that she could safely place her precious bundle down on the pastor's bed.

She felt perfectly at ease doing so . . . her daughter was so beautiful . . . yet no bed was too good for her to lie on . . .

As Maren fussed with her daughter's fancy semi-European outfit for the occasion, she looked over in deep wonder at the Christening gown to be worn by the Pastor's child—the long train and the fine little matching bonnet and the cradle where the little blonde Pastor's daughter slept the sleep of the innocent.

She went back into the parlor followed by the ever stout Johanne-Marie, whose resolute footsteps resounded far more across the Danish floorboards than hers ever did. Ojanna[6] knew her way around the homes of the Danes, for she had been coming and going in the Danish Colony families' houses for years.

Acting as hostess, the Minister's wife seated her Greenlandic guests at table and then directed her younger servant, who was related to Daniel and Maren to serve and entertain them. As family, she would also be bearing the Greenlandic child for the Christening ceremony and therefore she was dressed for the occasion in traditional white ceremonial furs decorated with pearls which rattled from her elbow every time she reached over to lift the coffee from its warming plate, and every time she gestured generously across the table to her guests to enjoy the dishes laid out on the Pastor's fine luncheon table. Since he had already eaten, Kateket, also a Greenlander, rose as everyone arrived to be seated, and retired into the Pastor's private study.

In the bedroom, the Pastor's wife dressed in a black silk gown which she had not worn

6. *Local Greenlandic pronunciation in the Colony for Johanne is made by grabbing the first vowel and putting it in front of any initial consonant. The h sound is also difficult to enunciate so is usually omitted. This modification is thus a shortening of the initial sound Jo/ or Yo/ to O/. Thus Louise would be Uluisa and John becomes Ojoth.*

The Two Elses

for over a year since their going away party at home with her parents and siblings . . . Oh yes, so many hundreds of miles now lay between them, but the joy of this occasion should keep her spirits from falling . . . despite the fond memories of family and friends so far away.

She took the little white silken bonnet and tied it prettily under her chin. A delicate blue veil gave her a poetic, dainty look where it was tied at the back of her neck.

"*Kussaktak,*" with their love of nicknames, is what the Greenlanders called her. The locals had named her after the dainty little shoreline bird that migrated back to Greenland every spring.

✦

The Church at the Nose

Down at the point, the Church is beautiful in its utter simplicity. Inside, above the altar next to the candlesticks and the chalice are twin cherubs in relief flanking both sides of Jesus on the Cross. Sunbeams pour down through the eastern bowed windows weaving their way past the altar gates, pews and the Baptismal Font.

The service was held for the Danes that Sunday in Danish and the Pastor's sermon was inspiring as usual. Yet the little Pastor's wife, who usually felt so uplifted at her husband's solemn words, was unable to concentrate on the lesson from the Gospels, and her thoughts kept wandering to the great moment when her daughter would be welcomed into God's Holy Kingdom, accompanied by the crescendo of chords from organ pipes, when words of the Christening psalm burst forth—then the moment itself arrived and the song rang out . . .

> *The Lord reaches out his embrace*
> *Blessing his little lambs*
> *He gathers us together in this*
> *   holy place*
> *That we may follow in his ways*
> *Blessed by holy waters clean*
> *Born again to us he brings*

The Two Elses

Waters from the source of life itself
Never will death or judgment fail
To bring us back when we have
gone astray . . .

The Greenlandic mother carried her child with equal conviction and reverence, without sentimentality; she did not press her babe to her heart or dot kisses on its forehead when the child's Godmother gently returned the bundle to her mother's lap. She simply wrapped her up in the blankets and quilt, even more carefully than before. Meanwhile, leather-clad singers, in their native dress, along with seminary students[7] and catechism pupils gathered around the organ, singing "Father take your child to your bosom," the final song for the newly baptized infants.

✦

The two Elses grew up side by side, first in their *Aamauten,* which are the leather packs for carrying babies worn by nannies on their backs.

The nannies were a pair of beautiful full-grown Greenlandic girls who competed to outdo each other in the fine art of decorating the *Aamauten* bags, one swearing by her soft sealskin, the other proudly flourishing her white reindeer hides. When she noticed a certain light blue veil streaming out from the Danish child's pack, stylishly wrapping itself around the "Chinese" hairstyle of the first nanny, the second nanny, caretaker for the Greenlandic Elserak, would steam in jealous envy.

The travelling troop of nannies and babies would often stop along the Colony road to visit Godmother Buck, the Magistrates wife, who always wanted to have a little peek at the two bundles under all those blankets inside the *Amaut* hoods. It wasn't long before the Pastor's child was a required source of entertainment for the childless Magistrate's family.

Upon arriving for a little visit at their house, Cook would announce to the household that the child had come, then the best of fur carpets would be rolled out, along with giant soft pillows, balls of yarn, even Godfathers' best sea lion hat would be tossed into the mix. Godfather and Godmother were not beneath a playful romp with the baby, prepared to act as Big Doggie, Sea Lion, or even Mr. Polar Bear. Of course the little "lamb" was allowed to tug at Godfather's beard and pull Godmother's hair.

7. *Students at the Lutheran Seminary, the only one in Greenland, were recruited along with novices from many remote areas north and south. After a long training lasting up to six years, they were sent out to many parts of Greenland to sing at services.*

The Two Elses

When she was one and a half years old, little Elserak became a true Greenlandic girl, according to her father Daniel, when she was given her first pair of embroidered leggings, even though they were hardly longer than a hand's length, as well as her first anorak, and strong reinforced knee boots. This ritual even included her hairstyle, which was swept up to form a top knot, despite its short length, displaying her colorful headband as the final step in her total transformation from a child outside the ring of Greenlandic community to inside. Despite her small stature, she almost seemed aware of the heritage which this costume represented and the ensuing responsibility for it which she would carry to her final days. Indeed, the light-hearted and jovial Greenlandic people seemed to grow from the seeds of a serious and contemplative infancy.

Whether you were a king or a pauper, this was a day to be remembered in the life of the Greenlanders, a day of celebration. As the proud father, Daniel played the host, generously pouring coffee for everyone. Godfather Buck, not to be outdone, added to the festivities by sending for Old Maren, the official Colonial Queen of Coffee, to brew and serve it along with sweets and tobacco, all at his expense. The Greenlanders were delighted at the additional party fare and word was sent to the Danes to come down to Bucks. The little golden curled "lamby" had spent most of her day there anyway, until she finally fell asleep on Godfather Buck's big bed, which she often did. So many times had she fallen asleep there, that one night her parents actually walked home without her, forgetting that she was still sleeping in Buck's big bed!

The gray day that had dawned in that month of December had an unusual leaden sky heavy with vast amounts of snow ready to fall. The days leading up to it had been so unseasonably warm and calm just before, that it came to be called "the calm before the storm."

The men were sitting outside softening and stretching their rawhides on the iron tipped wooden block and the women were complaining about the price of meat and their servants' clumsiness when suddenly the explosive sound of a fierce driving wind banged the storm shutters against the windows in the parlor. The loud banging and drumming of the wind turned into a sound like a gunshot, reminding the partying Danes that life is not always fun and games with birthday parties late at night in the middle of a Greenlandic winter. The Magistrate leaped up with an oath and wanted to rush outside, but Cook Daniel stopped him in his tracks. Daniel pleaded with everyone to go straight home before the storm made it impossible. Nobody was in the mood to leave, but they had to, as the Magistrate himself stood up and directed everyone to obey his orders for the sake of safety. In the blink of an eye everyone was ready to go, the

The Two Elses

door was opened and . . . Oh no! How terrible!

It was hard to find words to describe what they saw. The demonic whirlwinds outside howled and the complete white-out conditions poured into the hallway, even through the tiniest cracks. After a while the door was opened a second time to look, and it was impossible, for the ladies especially—it was clear they had no other hope but to stay put where they were, which was exactly what the men wished they could do as well, but what about the three wives at home waiting for their husbands to return home from the party?

Karen, Maren and Mette, along with their respective families, would be anxiously waiting for their return. The Greenlanders are afraid to stay alone in the Danish houses, especially when the weather was bad. The chimney whines, the slate roof groans, the doors in the attic bang open and shut—it all sounds so supernatural and terrifying! The servants should not be abandoned, so the front door had to be opened one last time—third time is the charm, right? With Daniel the Cook in the lead, and the young volunteers as wingmen, the men poured out into the blinding white blizzard of darkness. Only by listening to the direction of the howling wind, which was doubly fierce at the harbor, could they find their way home. The brave young volunteer who had joined the men more out of a lust for adventure and good sport, and who at first did not play a necessary role in the operation, did return after many hours to tell the Buck household that most of the men had made it back to their families safely.

However, when the Magistrate's youngest servant came out of her house to go to work the next morning, she found the snow as deep as a man is tall outside the door of the house. Daniel the Cook had not been out with his early morning chores to shovel a path through the snow as usual. He had ended up in a snow cave which he had dug himself down into during the blizzard, far away from the village. He had become quite turned around in the whiteout conditions the night before. He had mistakenly drifted past the entrance to his own cottage during the blizzard and never found his way back home, going further and further away from the settlement.

Dawns early light brought a pause in the wind allowing him to see where he was, and he barely made it back home alive to his wife and family. Others that morning disappointed the Magistrate and his guests by leaving *them* in their far more comfortable situations in the aftermath of the great blizzard.

✦

The Two Elses

The two Elses grew up to become two adventurous young girls, full of life. One with big brown eyes, the other with long lashes and eyes of blue; one with the broad nose of the Greenlanders, the other with a cheeky turned-up nose.

During the summer months, they were inseparable on berry walks and fearless explorations through the purple hillsides of heather, heath and gorse. In the long winter they could be seen sledding together on sewn-up skins, sometimes with a brave fellow in the back to steer, who would gallantly grab the shoulders of one of the damsels when he himself was about to lose his balance, or even worse, he would flip up over their heads on purpose to impress them. More often than not, the two girls were alone. The sight of Danish Else, dressed in her woolen winter snow suit trimmed with fur framing her face struggling to get her sled in its tracks, her sleeves stuffed so tight she could barely bend her elbows, her fur trimmed mittens reaching down to paddle her sled through the snow, fit the picture a true little Eskimo far closer than the Greenlandic child who, in contrast, could be seen in ordinary clothes with a red headscarf blowing in the wind, looking like some storybook heroine! Sometimes they would switch roles, however, and the Greenlandic child would take charge like a little thundering Napoleon with a brisk tongue barking orders which were passively followed by the gentle and sensitive

Dane, whose compliance bordered on weakness. Surprisingly, Else Holm grew stronger and more skilled from her playmate's rough games. Through them, she also learned the ways of the Greenlanders, which made her quite popular among them.

Danish Else learned how to chew seal blubber (*tamorask*) with the best of them, not to mention the dried seal jerky (*nigguts*), and she gladly dipped her biscuits in rendered seal oil. In the Greenlandic cottages she swapped clothes with Else Daniel and other Greenlandic children when she needed to. She sang lullabies for an army of drowsy dolls and infants sleeping in leather *Amauts* she "borrowed," and her favorite game of all was to crawl inside a giant *Amaut* bag and take a nap—something her mother would never approve of if she knew of it.

Saturdays at the Godparents' house were the best of all the days of the week for play time. The girls were spoiled with bags of delicious nuts, freshly baked cookies, and a big doll whose body was made in the Greenlandic cottages, but whose perfect wax head came from across the sea, sent after their first birthday by a Danish auntie.

There were real painting sets which both godparents used for painting landscapes while they told stories about the scenes in front of them. They shared tales of gorgeous ladies dancing in gowns at balls, of brides, waterfront cities

The Two Elses

with bridges and promenades, flowering meadows and windmills on every hill above deep blue skies. Godmother explained that this was the magical land of "Oresund" in Denmark. After a few of these Saturdays, Elserak was not always quite as kind towards her Danish friend (childhood jealousy!). She would often tease Else by saying Godmother was *ajorpok*, or unkind towards Greenlanders, just like the other Colonial ladies. Else was confused by this, and would stand frozen in front of her friend not knowing what to do about it. To top it off, Elserak would stick out her tongue and run away. Soon they would recover from these spats and the pair could be seen hand in hand, running together down the central road singing silly songs like "Geerts Lovesick Song" or the comic "The Magistrate who never learned how to paddle a kayak." Another favorite was the classic children's song which highlighted the Greenlandic colonial dilemma with its ending chorus of "You better behave and be quiet or the Big Bad Danes will come and get you!" (*Allalarsuit*)

However, in some way, Else Daniels had been correct in her perceptions about Godmother Buck. Mrs. Buck had not made many inroads in the Greenlandic community compared to other Danish women; she struggled to see beyond the outer appearances of the two girls, and she had never spent any time in the homes of local Greenlandic families.

In other ways the Magistrates as a couple were well-liked by the folks down in the village and it was a sad summer day—the girls being in their eighth year—when the yard in front of the Magistrates House was strewn with straw, packing crates, and moving boxes. Cook bustled about barking orders as all the personal items from inside the house were carried out and packed down for shipping. Finally, one day there was the ominous cry of "Boat from the North!" a shout which meant the same as, "now our dear old Buck's would be loading up and leaving us for good!"

So the Bucks departed to be replaced by the Sorensens and their big boy Frederick who quickly became a steady playmate for the Elses. From early morning to late in the day, the children played on the hillsides or at the "Fat House Nose" landing near the boatyard. They tumbled around stacks of lumber or helped the boat builder with his repairs, sometimes gathering wood shavings into sacks to be distributed around the Greenlandic houses in the village. Frederick especially loved to help old Rasmussen the blacksmith by pulling the bellows while the girls would fly in and out of his smithy in their attempts to drag him back into their games. The carefree days flew by, and time seemed to stand miraculously still as the girls knew nothing of sorrow—as far as Else Holm knew, sorrow was something people invented

The Two Elses

in far away places—there was certainly nothing called sorrow in existence in Greenland, at least not here in the Colony!—and in that belief she lived until one morning in the New Year after her father's return from Church services, his face unusually cross. Instead of giving her a gentle kiss on the cheek he brushed right past her and went straight up to his study, followed by her good friend the blacksmith. Loud and angry voices rang out from the study and then they came out. Her father had tears in his eyes and was showing signs of brotherly affection towards the smith, patting him on the shoulders and such, which seemed at odds with the sounds she had just overheard.

Else was very saddened by this event; for the first time she was struck by a deep feeling of inner pain and she believed that this must be the kind of "sorrow" that people talked about.

She grew more serious from that day forward, and she was no longer able to laugh with Elserak over the halfway or entirely intoxicated "Colonists"[8] who could be seen making a spectacle of themselves along the main Colony road—especially on holidays—putting on a bit of a show that was more sad than funny.

She could only guess that her smith had taken part in some aspect of the drunken revelry along with the other Greenlanders, and then showed up drunk at church that fateful morning in January.

Yet his star did not necessarily fall, in her eyes, with this one lapse in judgment. "Old Rasmussen," without knowing of it or why, was quickly forgiven, and his behavior grew unwittingly more virtuous, revealing a softness for poetry, rather than spirits—especially verses dedicated to his dear friend the Moon. For it was the moon who kindly lit his path in the darkness at night as he stumbled from the cottages to his home. Elserak on the other hand, did not understand a single word of the singing smith's rhyming poetry, such as "drunk-skunk, sky-fly, or moon-spoon," but that lack of comprehension did not keep her from roaring out in song as she marched, arm-in-arm, up and down the Colony road in the afternoons. Hanging above the grassy hills, hidden by a high outcropping, the moon itself was waiting for the moment to reign supreme over the evening light, washing the heavenly skies of their greenish dusky shades, green from her battle with the Day. Else, the Pastor's daughter, was especially fond of the quality of the light at this time of day here on the waterfront of the "Nose." When the Blacksmith stood in his doorway with his pipe between his teeth, gallantly tipping his hat down

---

8. *Colonists refer in this context to native Greenlanders working for the Colonial Administration.*

The Two Elses

to her, she always returned his exaggerated courtesy with a heartfelt nod of unspoken mutual understanding. Elserak, on the other hand, full of mischief, could not stop herself from laughing irreverently at the man. He, on the other hand, acknowledged his deep affection for his "little lady" by fashioning a perfect model of a real clothes iron for her birthday, the finest creation he had ever made. That winter the smith took a fall and broke his leg on the icy Colonial road.

◆

Two years passed.

Two little girls, one Danish, one Greenlandic, sat together talking.

"My grandmother really went to Denmark when she was younger as a nanny for *Mamakakas*," said the Greenlandic girl with pride. The Danish girl was hardly impressed by such a boast, since she had been there herself.

"But our country is so much better than yours," the Greenlandic girl continued, "because grandmother told us that you can't put your foot down anywhere without stepping onto someone's else's private property—either the King or somebody already owns everything—whereas here you are allowed to pick berries or gather

Qvaner[9] leaves wherever you please without worrying about trespassing from north to south and you don't have to pay for it either."

"And in Denmark," she persisted stubbornly," nobody dares drink a single drop from the tiniest brook without having to pay for it, or risk being thrown into prison!" She tossed her head vehemently, her pony tail dancing merrily atop her crown.

"So, you believe we actually have little brooks in Denmark, do you?" replied the Dane, gathering her wits for equal combat, "what about our springs, and fountains, maybe even golden apples—have *you* ever seen that?"

"No," Those notions lay beyond the imagination of the other girl, even though she tried her hardest, it was impossible for her to dress up her native Greenlandic fruit in golden hues in her mind's eye. The closest she could think of was the time when Danish Else's mother had sorted some fruit in the yard outside the Pastor's house from a recent Danish shipment, to the joy of all the local Greenlandic children who ran to grab the edible treasure, so rare and priceless..... what sort of magical country was Denmark really, where her grandmother had gone, where such unimaginable fruit could grow on trees?

---

9. *A great, beautiful umbrella plant that is edible.*

The Two Elses

Pastor Holmes had returned with his family from his two years away in the homeland. Mrs. Holmes could not endure the thought of resisting the misguided temptation, which many Danes indulged in, of shipping fruit to their friends in far away Greenland, causing some commotion among the Greenlanders at the strange sights—like "giant yellow berries" otherwise known as apples, for the privileged few to consume.

Up on Flag Pole Hill the Pastor's daughter sat with her Greenlandic friend once again, and they debated the merits of their respective lands of origin, since Danish Else has just returned from her trip to Denmark. Danish Else was very happy to be reunited with her beloved hills and the freedom she enjoyed there, which she had so bitterly longed for when she was away, especially at first, when she stayed in the crowded city. She took in the vast views of her dear brown hillsides all dressed in purple heather, surrounded by stern iron clad mountains of the inland ranges with their snowy white caps—and how cheery was the song of the brook against the wind in the trees behind the Pastor's house! But still, she would not allow Elserak to get away with making fun of her homeland in Denmark.

As they were chatting away softly up on the hillside, a cheery boy's voice called up to them in Greenlandic, "...but where did you go, Elserak?"

It was Frederick, who preferred the company of Greenlandic Else for all his adventures, both "by land and by sea," through sleet and snow, through thick and thin.

At the sound of his voice, Elserak jumped up to join Frederick, while the Danish Else was sadly left behind—she was jealous to find how quickly she was abandoned by her friend; but she had a charming book at the house which she ran down to get, and with it under her arm she settled into a heather-lined hollow in the outcropped rocks. Small birds hopped around her, and the sun cast down white rays of light across the ocean below. Notes of a jolly sailor's shanty wafted up from the decks of a long boat that was unloading down in the shipping harbor. As the first few tears began to roll down her cheeks for the "Poor Old Tom" in her book, a "poaching archer" stuck his head up over the crest of the hill, but then pulled himself out of her sight just as quickly. It was Frederick, who had had a falling out with his sweetheart. She had run home to her family cottage in a bad mood. He pretended not to care, and continued hunting small birds with his bow and arrow.

Else Holm waved to him and he quickly came over, but not before she had smoothed down her skirts over her legs, which he stared at with great admiration. He had never seen a pair of legs like that; white stockings and light canvas footwear with . . . heels? He had only seen

The Two Elses

kamikker. (Both Danes and Greenlanders wore *kamikker* universally.)

Did he know this Uncle Tom? No, but it sounded like a great book. She suggested he read it and she did, right there and then, from the beginning. Perhaps he did not care for the translation? Nobody could blame him for that. His reasons for throwing the book down with a look of what appeared to be disgust were not clear . . . however, his opinion of the girl who had brought the book up there, that was another story altogether. It certainly did not lower her value in his eyes when she declared that she truly wished she was wearing her old *kamikker* instead of her ridiculous Danish boots, for then she would be able to easily race him all the way down to the bottom of the steep hillside cliffs and the sea shore. Her *kamikkers*, thank goodness, were being repaired under the deft hands of Elserak's mother, known to be the best seamstress in the place.

It was only a few days later that they were on her feet, for the occasion of the seasonal highland walk for all ages and capabilities, both young and old, big and small, to Little Malene's Peak about a two hour march up from the Colony.

Oh how truely wonderful it was to walk through the hills and valleys, the Greenlanders always a fair bit ahead, despite the fact that they were loaded down like elephants, carrying plenty of provisions to ensure the Danish necessary comfort. The Danes panted and struggled up the footpaths from the very start even though they had only themselves to carry. This provided a great deal of amusement among the Greenlanders, though all in all, everyone was in high spirits due to the natural beauty everywhere and the gorgeous summer weather. Across the heather filled meadows and hillsides, echoes of laughter and spirited shouts of joy, along with the report of a rifle shot now and again.

"Give me a hand, dear Elisif, crossing this stream—I'm about to fall in!" begged the corpulent Magistrate who thought that Elses' name came from the formal Elisif. The little Else leapt nimbly from stone to stone to the rescue. From an outcropping above them, the light-footed doctor then proceeded to recite the entire ballad of Elisif, otherwise known as "Hercules at the Ford."

Another shot rang out and one of the porter men appeared with a pair of shepherds dressed in summer gear. They successfully ascended the peak of "Little Malene." Far below them the Colony lands stretched out like brown painted paper as the warm sun played across the light blue ocean stretching far beyond the furthest islands. Behind the tourists towered even taller mountain caps reaching into the clouds. It was almost as if the swirling mists up there were

The Two Elses

trying to hide winter's frozen glacial lakes and icy crags from the visitors as they enjoyed their summer adventure. A tent was put up for shelter against the cooler breezes billowing down from the glacier above. The Colony cooks had accompanied them. They browned steaks and boiled water while the housewives set the table on the uneven tent floor, arranging the most comfortable seats for the men—at least for those who had not literally thrown themselves down in the middle of everything, which prevented anyone from fixing them a more suitable and appropriate resting spot.

A few wanted to keep on hiking further up the steep escarpment; the doctor, who loved these expeditions more than anything, along with a few fellows who couldn't get enough of these hikes in the mountains, especially the rugged peaks above timberline, as opposed to the gentle slopes of the moss and heather covered valley floors.

"We just want to go up a little further!" they cried enthusiastically, to the dismay of those comfort seeking creatures staying behind in the tent, who begged them to return by the time the potatoes had finished boiling and not a second longer.

The Danish children and Elserak ran ahead in high spirits with some Greenlandic children in their tailwinds who tagged along uninvited. The tent was not large enough to fit everyone, so a few had to find shelter in the tent vestibule.

It was a lively scene there on the peak of Little Malene Mountain; everyone's mood soared to the happiest possible; there were endless toasts and bottles from both breweries, Tuborg and Carlsberg, were emptied with vigor. For the easy-going and indulgent folks, the tasks of life were simple, and life was good. Soon you could hear, "Ahh, the Sourdough bread!"

"Pass the mustard,". . . "Oh if you would be so kind as to send the cheese down here, my dear Fru Plum, you are sitting right next to it," to which she replies with a tart, "If you call this sitting then help yourself, here is the cheese!" "Ha! That was a lovely piece of salmon dear Mrs. Sorensen, did you get it from Kapsilik?"—

"So-so baetle!"[10] the children were singing outside.

"So, so wie ich Dich liebe—pass me a 'Jew Cake,' mother!" the doctor shouted.

"Think its time for a smoke?" asked someone from the group that had been waiting the longest. One fellow, fresh just off the boat and experiencing Greenland for the first time asked "My God! Do you think it's wise to light up in a tent?"

10. *Words from a children's singing game that sounds like "London bridge is falling down . . ."*

The Two Elses

The ladies laughed, "Well, here, anything can happen . . ."

They enjoyed the company of the men when they were in a good mood, and smoking certainly lifted their spirits. The party was a splendid success, as all the summer picnics to Mt. Malene had been.

The guests rose as the meal was officially declared completed, and everyone who was not packing things up could take their after dinner aperitif's to a favorite scenic viewing spot, as directed by one of the hostesses. "Who wouldn't love to see such a view then?" said one. "Does anyone have pen and ink?" another asked. "No but I've brought a sketchbook and pencils," shouted a third.

A page was torn out and all the names, including those of the children, were penned in; each one wrote an inscription, the sheet was rolled up tightly and placed inside an empty bottle, corked and stuffed in a crack for future generations to discover. Someone suggested a jig, but Sorensen felt it too warm, so nothing came of that, and instead he offered to host a gathering in his workshop that evening. Cheers went up from the Greenlandic girls in response.

Yet, as Cook Daniel liked to say, "When Men go looking for God they find him . . ." and that is exactly what happened. There was to be no dancing that day, but the unknowing Frederick Sorensen had plenty of important surprises awaiting him at the bottom of the hill . . .

Frederick's parents, unlike the other Danes living in Greenland, believed that their son might amount to something without the need of leaving home. They practiced this notion by keeping the boy at home to train him for one of the posts available in Greenland. That evening, the American Ben Jenkins arrived on a steam ship. He spent eight days in the Colony, drinking toddies after dinner with men from the leading families. That last evening, with sentimental tears of happiness flooding his eyes, he embraced the Colony magistrate heartily, as a prelude to his serious objections regarding the way the Sorensens were burying the talents of their boy in the isolation of Greenland.

Jenkins eventually received permission to take the boy to America and launch his career there. When the ship "Virginia" raised her anchor a few days later, Frederick waved goodbye with the quaint straw hat made by his mother from straw she had almost thrown away last year during unpacking, and which she was lucky enough to finish before the ship sailed.

"I'll come back to Greenland as soon as I have become a true sea-cadet!" the boy shouted to his proud, but sad parents on shore—the same parents who were convinced that they would *never* have to let him go! But who can see into the future?

Frederick had said his bashful goodbyes to the two Elses in private behind the Pastor's goat

The Two Elses

shed and, in turn, they had promised him "eternal friendship."

Now both girls stood back on the beach watching the smoke from the steamer's chimneys fade away with their friend to far, unknown places.

Several kayaks followed him through the archipelago, and he kept busy shouting down to his old friends from the elevated position he had reached on the "American's" deck. When the final moment came for his Greenlandic entourage to depart from the steamship's side, he pulled a page out of his notebook, wrapping his penknife in it as a token of remembrance for his best friend Rasmus, the grandson of Rasmussen the blacksmith.

Rasmus was the son of the smith's daughter, born and raised in a remote spot in the backcountry. He suffered from chronic dizziness when paddling kayak, and so could not earn a living on the water. Because of that, his grandfather brought him to the Colony to be apprenticed to the boatyard carpenter at "Fat House Nose," where he now worked as a full fledged Journeyman carpenter.

The two Elses honored Frederick's departure by singing the melancholy old "Ballad of Geert" from morning to night, inserting Frederick's name for Geert's. This went on for some time until Mrs. Holm forbade the singing inside her house, as it made her so sad.

> *When Gert[11] went away*
> *He cried and sang and he said*
> *Goodbye my people, goodbye*
> *From boyhood till manhood*
> *I loved every place I stood*
> *The beaches and hills and the sea*
> *Goodbye my people, Good Bye!*

A year later, on the anniversary of his departure on the "Virginia," they received letters from Frederick. He wrote that he was homesick and longing for his beloved Greenland and missed everyone—this he made clear from the start—especially "as he waved good-bye to his two dear friends on the shore, embraced by the dear hills of heather and heath . . ."

He described his hard times at sea through storm and squall, but now he was settled, living in Halifax. His new house-father had left to go whaling in Greenland. He had visited Washington, "a great and impressive city—extremely

---

11. *Geert or Gerhard was a Greenlandic boy who left during an era when it was rare for a native Greenlander to leave his homeland, compared to modern times. He never returned but was buried in Danish soil, compounding his sad story, which is chonicled in this poetic elegy or ballad expressing the feelings of many Greenlanders longing to return. The melody of this song is also especially beautiful.*

The Two Elses

hot, but with vast amounts of apples," this last observation being for the benefit of both Elses.

He had written letters to others in the Colony as well; to Assistant Moe, with additional "warm greetings to the Doctor's fiancé' Kisten, who he hoped had become Mrs. Moe by then." At this, the Assistant scratched his head a bit, puzzled. He would not have minded if it was in fact the case, but the beautiful Kisten was not that easily won over . . . so far.

There were other letters for Steffan Egede, the Magistrate's Cook, the Blacksmith, and a few others. Frederick had sent greetings to every Greenlander in residence by name, which made him *pitak,* a fine and great fellow. In his letter to his own parents, Frederick wrote in detail about the many characteristics of his new house-parents, especially their goodness and prosperity. He included photographs of various sizes that showed him with badges of honor as a decorated seaman, smoking cigars and wearing finger gloves. But throughout all his commentary, Frederick's homesickness for Greenland and all his people stood out undeniably. His mother cried as she read this, but soon next year she could dry her tears. Between each line, she also read the joy he felt at the thought of returning home. How wonderful it would be to receive a new and very interesting son—who had learned more about the world, who had new experiences under his belt.

"A year can fly by just as quickly as a day," thought Mrs. Sorensen," if he works hard, he might even return wearing the uniform of a decorated officer!"—Their hopeful ambitions for his greater success helped ease the daily sadness left by his long absence. However, as time went by, nothing quite followed the course they had all expected.

Life in Greenland for the two Elses was simple and free in the years that followed—like one long perfect summer day, not too hot or too cloudy.

✦

After a while Pastor Holm began to notice that his daughter had grown more "Greenlandic" and "Colonial" than he wished. His wife was less concerned; her little daughter's inborn gentility would override the "primitive" things she had picked up in her childhood. Yet when the Pastor made plans to send Else away to the Outback for a year to live under the influence of the very strict and formal Bucks, she supported the idea. Pastor Holm had written to the old Magistrate that "his daughter had become

The Two Elses

worldly and excessively free spirited, for what is suitable for the Greenlandic Amazons dressed in leather skins from top to toe, is totally unacceptable for the delicate Danish maiden . . ." as he put it with the ending flourish. Many times he had looked out his study window to see his delicate daughter plying carthorse to the giant Elserak, carrying her on her back while her legs sank helplessly into the snow. Terrible! Just like the story of the daughter of King Karl the Great and Egenhart. Things got even worse the next day, when the girl complained she had a sore throat, and so was bundled up with extra layers to keep the chill off. At her desk studying her geography lesson, she nodded off asleep, and out tumbled a tiny little puppy that had been inside her scarf and warm collar, which together made the perfect hiding spot for a little puppy. This little scene helped her father finalize his decision to send her away, for what else could he do? If they couldn't help, who else could? Ending on a note of desperation, the Pastor closed his letter to Governor Buck in the Outback and sent it with the postman. When he returned with mail a fortnight later, the "wild little Danish maiden" was running up and down the shoreline with all the Greenlandic children who rushed in to see if there was any news. She grabbed the waterproof kayak bag used by the mail carriers where the postman had left it to deliver other letters and small parcels to other Greenlandic residents which he had collected on his way back to the Colony. Else shook the mailbag hoping to discover its secret contents; there will certainly be a letter from her Godmother, but what would it say?

She ran and twirled ahead of the postman all up the road chattering in her native tongue about the outback and what it was like out there. Finally they reached the Magistrates house and the mail sack with all of its secrets could be opened. She found her letter, grabbed it and ran with Elserak to the Pastor's house. Soon everyone knew that Else the pastor's daughter would be headed to the outback to stay with the Bucks for many years to come.

"How many hours do you think Godmother will force me to practice every day?" asked Else Holm, with the theatrical notes of a martyr thrown in for good measure.

"*Kullinik*. At least ten!" answered Else Daniel with the confidence of a queen.

Godmother was known to be well-educated, and Else would certainly benefit from the arrangement, she believed. With this fine plan in place, her mother allowed Else to spend time all winter visiting her friends enjoying her favorite childhood pastimes, singing psalms with her Greenlandic friends and families, even caroling with a group under her parents' window one morning. On the eve of Three Kings Day she dressed up in her traditional Greenlandic cos-

The Two Elses

tume for the local mummer's play (somewhat out of context) just like all the local children. In February, during Carnival she went sledding with everyone in her leather sledding sack on the ski hill and wacked the empty barrel with her stick, as the custom calls for, even winning the grand prize of King Cat for the day, to her father's great dismay. She went up to receive her prize, which was a beautiful silk scarf donated by the Colonial office for the festivities. Mrs. Sorensen, the magistrate's wife, promised Else a grand party, a going away Ball. It was time for an elegant dance in the Magistrates house. Greenlanders had not been invited to dances there since the days of dear old *Mamakakske,* when the lady of the house was Greenlandic herself, and so would open her doors to everyone. She was of the old school, "come as you are," informal and impromptu.

Her parties would last till the wee hours of the morning. Everyone loved them, especially including the Magistrate himself. The children loved them as well, for they were never put to bed; they would fall over in a corner somewhere and nap for a while, then wake up and dance again when they felt like it. Harbor seal stew would be simmering in a big kettle on the stove in the corner, along with a bottomless coffee pitcher that brewed all night. Those were the days when life was good! The old folks who remembered stories would sigh in longing and the memories would begin ...

When friends and family came to say goodbye to Else, as they had for Frederick when he left long ago, they made an effort to dress up and make the day a festive one. Everyone would do their best and bring out their nicest clothes, leather kamikker, colorful woolens, cottons decorated with ribbons, pearls, bows, and shining buckles.

Fru Sorensen wanted the decorations to live up to the expectations of her guests, and, thinking of flowers, she came up with a substitution for the arrangements she would normally get from the boutiques of Copenhagen, now so far away. She borrowed cotton fabric and hung it up on the ceiling, interspersed with iconic pieces of hunting and fishing gear; rifles and bows with arrows; fishing nets, anchors, and the Danish flag. The shipyard carpenter made frames shaped like trees and she wrapped these in heather.

In addition, the carpenter worked with old Maren on a drum, a drum which Sorensen believed to be essential for the musicians. The Pastor house cook was lent out for the day of the party. Fru Holm believed that Else would have to wear white for her dance, and so she proceeded to take apart her summer curtains to create the right effect for her ball gown. The Doctor's wife, Kisten, who was a beauty like no other, and therefore naturally included on the

The Two Elses

guest list, wore a fur coat studded with pearls she borrowed from a local girl. Every day she had given this girl some of her Danish food at lunch time, and, since not everybody owns a pearl-studded fur coat, she had bought herself the right of borrowing it for one evening. As it is in any big town when a much anticipated event is in the works, the whole place at the *Spit* was abuzz with preparations and excitement as the day grew near.

Everything was ready. Lights and candles lit, Fru Sorensen came bustling out of the bedroom in her silken gown and fashionable cap festooned with baby-blue ribbons trailing down her back.

She looked around, smiling, satisfied.

The Greenlandic guests were huddled at the end of the long formal hallway near the front entrance, bashful at first to set foot over the doorway. The cook gave orders; "Come on then, come inside, will you?" Fru Sorensen, struck by a bolt of inspiration, called for a reel to break the ice and put everyone at ease. She was right of course, and soon all the Danes were there, children and domestics, at least those generally considered the most attractive and best-dressed girls suitable for attending such a ball.

One of the "lads" of the ball was feeling a bit too warm and disappeared for a short time, turning up again in short sleeves. Such a transgression of the unwritten rules was not permitted, and he was, in short order, informed by a translator that young Greenlanders were not expected to change their attire during the celebration. The dancer, having no desire to be excluded from the joys of the ball, and certainly not willing to forego the festive spread of appetizers offered at the buffet table, struggled quickly back into his heavy Greenlandic costume, the *anorak*.

The Danes were served in a room to the side. Their dishes were not limited to simple appetizers, but included a full and elegant dinner. When the dining drew to a close, the young people promenaded along the hallways as the dance floor was swept and rinsed down with vinegar, and the room was aired out.

The dancing resumed with a free, cavorting mood of delight that helped to dissolve the social barriers. The young women had dainty handkerchiefs which they used to pat their moistened brows, and mop the sweat off their partners' faces. These they stored discretely in their sleeves as they danced. The Magistrate himself grabbed the elbow of Elserak and steered towards a reel set, to her great mortification. She nearly had to be dragged up to dance, though a sea of dancers were jostling for an opportunity. The Greenlanders watching on the sidelines were bursting with laughter at the sight of Elserak dancing with the Magistrate, crying out "*illa kuijannavigpok*! Look how he is swinging her around, now

The Two Elses

he's lifting her clear up, look, her feet are off the ground!" As the couples sashay down the line Else takes small steps like a damsel in the days of chivalry—her knight at his milk-white steed, her soldier in his white spats—and she is laughing as she floats down the tunnel of clapping hands turning heads, laughing and stepping the figures she had learned long ago. The dance ended with a raucous shout as she is led out by her partner, despite the custom of ending a reel that brings the lady all the other partners, as if she was fleeing someone unpleasant.

Steffan's Epha and Rasmus, the blacksmith's boys, were the lucky friends of Frederick and this endeared them very much to Fru Sorensen. Her attentions to them soon spread to the others and their popularity at the dance grew. The Greenlanders, like everyone else, did not always respect someone because they had earned it, but rather had the habit of bestowing respect and admiration to those who enjoyed the respect of an important member of their community, since "everyone loves a winner."

Kateketen,[12] who was always able and ready for anything, called out a final toast for Mr. and Mrs. Sorensen after giving a heartfelt speech that expressed the sentiments held by everyone in the room. The Magistrate gave a speech for Else Holm, who wore a paper garland of small blue daisies made for her by her mother. This overwhelming moment of great honor was a novel experience for Else, who looked so sweet as she raised her glass in thanks, her eyes wet with the tears she was holding back.

Everyone wanted to bang on the new drum, a wondrous novelty for many living in the Colony who had never seen one before. It was no children's toy drum, which the Danish children at least knew, but a full sized percussion instrument. Finally the cooks brought out the coffee, but Greenlanders object to this subtle marker for the ending of the ball. They refuse to leave the dance lines, not even tempted by their favorite drink of all. The Magistrate's cook emerged with his voice of authority and sounded out the impressive Greenlandic, "*Soraniaitsegok*! The festivities are now concluded!"

The terrible words being spoken, the tired fiddlers knew just what to do to save the mood. They drew their bows to the tune of "Good Night Ladies" and followed up with a rousing fanfare to smoothly escort everyone on their way home. The ball was over and it was splendid, a celebration of happiness long to be remembered.

---

12. *or Vicar, under the tutelage of the Pastor.*

The Two Elses

♦

The ship Haien was ready to set anchor in the fjord and Else Holm was ready to depart. Her father had tied a dingy behind the steamer and sailed back home after three days at sea, about fifty miles north of the Colony.

It was the same spot where he stood fourteen years ago and received the news of his new paternity. The beach had been crowded with people wanting to say their last goodbyes to their darling Else. The Magistrate's cook came running with special treats packed for her trip from Fru Sorensen's kitchen. He had words of his own to share with her as well; Else should carry greetings to her ladyship Godmother and tell her that the cooks hat she had given him upon her departure was completely worn out! And don't forget to share warm greetings with Mekissok, his colleague in the north, "Don't forget Oles and Adams!" someone shouted to her. "And remember me to ..." They all shouted names for her to carry up north. Suddenly a voice called out, "And God Bless the young lady on her way ... " It was from someone standing up on a rock on the point where the steamer would be passing close by. It was the old smith Rasmussen, leaning on his staff.

After the Haien[13] had sailed away with her friend, Elserak went straight home where she sat on her bed in sorrow and mourned, as would naturally be expected. A few tears were shed into the hands that held her head, but they were quickly dried and soon she had other things to do and think about. First, there was the promise of an extra tour of the ship with sea shanties, accordion and fiddle tunes, then romantic walks in the hills above the harbor, then later a boat trip deep into the mouth of the fjord to the camp known as her Igdlunguak—a tour ending with her wintering over in new surroundings.

The little Igdlunguak has two cabins. The kayaks and boats wind their way between the break waters and across the surf after a storm that had lasted three days. The mountains rose up out of the fog and mist revealing a magical landscape with valleys and zebra stripped highland meadows tumbling down to a point reaching the seacoast.

The young men in their kayaks bobbing on the tall waves said that after the storm the sky and hills had the look of a human face that had once been furrowed and creased in anger, and was now smoothing out into an expression of peace and gentleness. It was a fitting metaphor for the land there. The little clearing was named

---

13. *"Shark."*

The Two Elses

after some abandoned ruins, now covered in tall grasses. Beautiful fjords and peninsulas reach their fingers out into the sea and green patches dot the hill tops where the ice had melted. The fragrant qvane plants grew in those green patches, to the joy and nourishment of all travelers.

Steffen Egede and Amalie had come here for many years since the seal hunting grounds were better for their three sons. Epha was the leader of the pack of harbor seal hunters. Life was full of the hunt now for friend Amalie—very different since the days when she could rest in the sun watching the little boys running after robbins with their bows and arrows. They needed far more than robbins to survive these days. Elserak's cousin Epha was the best hunter in the camp and everyone knew it. He looks handsome and powerful as he stands at the shore in his black and weathered storm gear of leather, salted down by sea-spray, his face framed by its deep hood, leaning on his kayak paddles telling stories to cousin Steffan. No wonder the young girls in the second house find excuses to go down to the shore and wait for a glimpse of him out on the water every afternoon when the hunters come home.

Today Epha had no seal meat from his hunt but he did bring back news of the Pastor's arrival as soon as the weather permitted. When the Pastor came, the festivities followed. Preparations for his visit began at once.

Amalie's house was just as tidy and clean as the house she ran in the Colony. She had beautiful new furs on the twin beds, nice wall lamps and small shelves along the walls to hold all the things she needed to prepare meals. The air in the living room was surprisingly good due to the installation of an air vent called the *kingak* (which means the "nose"), a traditional building practice which, unfortunately, has long since been forgotten by most Greenlandic builders. Even in the most well ventilated Greenlandic houses (we won't mention the worst cases) the air smells of a rank cross between hides and wet feathers.

This is overcome by two factors. First, enjoying the company of the good people you are with, and second, the necessity of survival by escaping the worse conditions outside. The food that is eaten inside these shelters is not easily enjoyed by anyone who is not Greenlandic, and they are tolerant of that fact. This is why few if any are invited inside, out of a tactful wish to avoid the issue. At the Igdlunguak camp where Steffan stayed, Danes had been there for generations and were easily accommodated. His wife took care of the Pastor when he finally arrived. She had a room ready for him where the children normally slept. In her house the floors were swept so clean you could not even find the tiniest mouse. A rare thing that was, which she knew was of great importance to the European taste, and unlike that of the Greenlanders. The Pastor found his bed, and his neighbor was Johanne-Marie, whose son-in-law had left the Colony. He has given his shops to a younger woman allowing him to live with his relatives closer to home. Johanne-Marie had not gained much in the way of beauty with the passing of years, but she could talk up a storm!

She had been cultivating some bitterness towards the Danes whom she felt were intruders in her land—a feeling with some justifiable merit. She did not hold back in the presence of the Pastor. "Ya, you Danes know so much more than us Greenlanders," she said, "but that God given knowledge which we have all received is exactly the same for everyone, but the way you Danes use yours is often very bad—even our primitive ancestors long ago, I have noticed, were far superior to you in their application of their God-given wisdom—they had more common sense!" To this, the Pastor inquired a bit further, but she replied, "Ya, I know it from that paper over there!" and she nodded towards her son-in-law.[14]

Steffan owned an old pamphlet that was so worn and used it was almost illegible. It contained fragments of Paul Egede's[15] Diary with many references to the time when small pox arrived in Greenland—*kuppit* it was called—a disaster which Johanne-Marie laid at the feet of the Danes. "For if *you* had not come to our land," she said, "then half our population would not have perished!"

"But if the Danes had not come to you," replied the Pastor, "then you would not have received Christianity."

"The Pastor is right!" an old hunter from the clearing nearby inserted. He had stopped by seeking shelter from the storm on his way home. When he heard that the Pastor was coming he stayed longer to visit. The Pastor was smiling as he read the tattered pages of the diary, laughing lightly at its contents.

"Are you laughing at the stupidity of my forefathers again?" asked the naive old woman.

The priest nodded dreamily and continued reading while the house filled up with neighbors and visitors. The old woman was told to let the Pastor be in peace, and he could not be moved from his spot. He knew the diary well from many a close read—he even had a copy himself at home and knew the order of the pages by heart.

---

14. *Nodding or looking in the direction of an object is considered the polite form of indicating something, as opposed to pointing.*
15. *Paul Egede was the son of the missionary Hans Egede and he continued his father's work.*

The Two Elses

As he scanned the familiar lines down the worn pages he exclaimed again, "Ah yes, dear Pastor, what you say is true enough—not dumb at all, but wise words coming from a so called healthen."

He was reading the passage where Paul Egede and his apprentice are in a conversation and the following question arises;

"Was the Danish King fairly good when it came to hunting the whale?"

"His oldest son (the Crown Prince), was he improving his fishing techniques?

"Does God know about the Dutch people?"[16]

"Greenlanders have known about the Dutch long before the little Pastor man arrived."

And the following humorous story about the printed pages of a book was the current source of laughter. The old man from up north who had been listening with delight squeezed his bony chest with spindly arms as he looked down at the paper . . .

"A heathen had stolen the Latin Grammar Book belonging to Hans Egede. He wanted his wife to sew him a new panel from its cloth cover for his finest fur coat. Paul Egede found out and tried to save a few pieces of his dear book cover and announced a reward for its return. He offered a linen shirt in exchange for his grammar book. No ordinary linen shirt, but a dress shirt to be worn on the outside in the fashion of those days. But the Greenlander, who felt guilty about the theft was also suspicious that a trap was being set for him with this reward and that they would know he had done it. He hid and if he saw anyone would only casually remark that the book was nothing but *ajorpok,* or dirt, and if his wife had tried to sew the cloth that bound it into his coat, it was so thin it would fall apart, being so thin and besides, it was not waterproof, and so would not do well in the rain."

"Well, what do you think about that, Johanne Marie?" asked the Pastor gently. The old woman's face showed a deep disdain for Egede's poor grammar.

The pastor had decided that his first day should be for resting and conversation with the Greenlanders. He suggested that they read from the manuscript but everyone suddenly felt bashful. So he read it out loud to them, which everyone enjoyed very much.

Like children, the Greenlanders always wanted to hear the stories they knew so well over and over again. But we have stopped paying attention to the old stories. The manuscript was placed inside Amalie's sewing basket and Steffan began to prepare for evening

---

16. *The Dutch had been trading walrus tusk with the Eskimo long before Hans Egede's time.*

The Two Elses

worship as the local catechist. The following day the Pastor held exams for the children and went over the accounting books which Steffan had prepared. The whole settlement came to chapel that evening which was held in Steffan's house, the largest of the two. Everyone worshipped by candlelight from small traveling candles brought by the Pastor, their rays shining through the small windows of Steffan's house. The western sky was aglow with the setting afternoon sun and the children, who were not allowed to take sacrament at the altar, gathered instead on the flat roof outside, joining in on the familiar church psalms. The singing streamed outwards from within and spread through the hills and valleys that seemed to be quietly listening. When the service was over the Pastor continued his journey visiting other households and camps in the Fjord. He was followed down to the boat by every one of the souls of his people of Igdlunguak, even out to sea some of the young boys, the sons of Isipiluk[17] paddled out in his wake, along with the old man who was already headed out to the further northern fjord.

✦

Elserak was connected to her homeland by the bonds of blood and her ancestors. While Else Holm played sonatas in the outback, Greenlandic Else learned the ways of her people from Uncle Steffan. She learned how to gut seals, clean, scrape and process the skins, and make beautifully embroidered garments from the leather. Towards the end of winter she had made a fine pair of kayak mittens for Steffan, with thumbs well sewn for good paddling, that detail being essential for the hunters, and they were at least as good, if not better than, any others made in those parts.

For Else, staying at Igdlunguak was part of her education and introduction to life itself; just as "going away" was for the Danish Colony children. Boys and girls could plant the seeds for their future, counting on some of these experiences somehow bearing fruit later in life. In the course of one winter, Elserak had grown in her maturity as far as any young Greenlandic woman could be expected. Her reading was limited to assigned schoolbooks, and her skill at handwork hardly changed once she had learned all the basics. It wasn't until she reached the age of motherhood, with all its joys and sorrows, that new thoughts began to take root for her.

17. *The one with poor eyesight.*

The Two Elses

At first she longed for the excitement of life in the Colony, and was bored in the solitude of the winter camp. Cousin Epha, five years her senior, was always encouraging her to show more patience and thoughtfulness. Once, he said, "People are like gardens, like those gardens the Danes talk about at home (Greenlanders did not have gardens). Weed your garden, and you will see the fruits of you labors!" She knew exactly what he meant, but she was not quite ready to give up her sour moods for the better art of "weeding."

◆

Sisemiut, or Foxhole land in the Outback, is considered by many to be the most desirable of the six south Greenlandic Colonies. If one desires to never meet a solitary soul, other than the Greenlanders, then this may be considered true. During the greater part of the year, no stranger ever set foot in this remote area, and if they do it is only known in the dimmest seal blubber lamplight. If absence of people defines desirability, this remote place was certainly one of the best. Many also say this landscape was the most beautiful, though others would say that distinction belonged to Seal Point or Juliannehaab.[18]

Foxhole land was certainly full of beauty on many levels. In the summer, the brilliant green patches along the craggy cliffs and steep mountain meadows behind the Parsonage contrasted sharply with the jagged, somber ice capped peaks of the inland mountains. Along the steep green valleys, little mountain brooks dart down the rocks to the seashore where Greenlanders and Colonials are busy with summer work—storing new shipments of cargo and the like. Above the Danish houses, the flag waves cheerily to incoming ships from the whitewashed flagpole against the green fields. The dock at Seal Point was further away from the Colony's steep cliffs, but here the ship can sail in much closer and is nestled right up against the settlement. It is a festive sight in a place that traditionally stays on the quiet side—especially to see cook running towards the ceremonial cannon with coals in his steel tongs to light and fire the cannonball in greeting, then shouts "Welcome!" to mark the official arrival of summer's Danish visitors, as the ship drops anchor.

18. *Qaqortoq, formerly Julianehab, is a town in the Kujalleq municipality in southern Greenland. With a population of 3,229 in 2013, it is the most populous town in southern Greenland and the fourth largest town on the island.*

The Two Elses

During our time there, the number of Danes living in southern Greenland was at its lowest. There was a childless Magistrate, an unmarried Pastor, and an Assistant married to a Greenlander, who was himself part Greenlandic, and so preferred the company of his wife's friends. The Colonial Magistrate and his wife, known as "Godfather and Godmother," did not enjoy the local beauty of the countryside as much as others did. "I feel so hemmed in by towering mountains on one side and the immense fjords on the other," the substantial wife would complain. "Give me the views of open sea at Seal Point! There it seemed like only a few low sand bars lay between us and our motherland of Denmark!" And "Godfather" himself seemed to carry a similar longing.

So how did they pass the time in this place?

They threw themselves into great things—great things such as hunting for whales! The big prize there was all about whale hunting. This and only this was their primary focus—investing as fast as possible in every way to turn the Colony around with the help of whaling, eventually spreading the success to all of Greenland.

Destiny had other plans for them, however, and things turned out quite differently.

Year after year passed, whaling grew less and less important, and Godmother began to build a new foundation, becoming part of her new landscape, until she swore she would never leave, would never trade it for anywhere else, and she certainly wanted no one to join her there, to spoil it for her, she declared with aplomb.

Life had settled into a pleasant rhythm of habits and daily routines that included the dearly beloved local Pastor. So much so, that when they did receive the request from Pastor Holm to have Else boarding with them, it took some effort to imagine the loss of the comfort of their privacy, which previously would not have been an issue at all. Godmother would have been more than pleased to have such a distraction when she first arrived, but with the passing of time the natural tendency towards self-sufficiency had begun to set in and she had become complacent and narrow-minded. That was one of the greatest dangers of isolation in the Colony. Else's arrival changed all that—Godmother would be forced to think of someone else's welfare, there would be new tasks and duties to accomplish every day ... Of course a friendly letter to the Holms, accepting their request, must be sent back, which was gratefully received, as we have learned.

Else's new life was soon ordered in lessons for her schooling along with other activities to keep her busy. She soon felt at peace in her heart and soul and the comfort of that gave her great happiness.

On Sundays after Church Else wrote in her journal about the few weekly events that had transpired, for her parents. They read these en-

The Two Elses

tries with great interest, not so much to know what she had been busy with, but to gain some insight into their daughter's growing maturity and inner development.

Around one o'clock the Pastor usually stopped by Godfather's for dinner. Afterwards, Godfather took a silent hour of "self-reflection" as he called it, on the day bed. Everyone in the household enjoyed this peaceful hour according to his or her own desire. At three in the afternoon, the housemaid, dressed in her Sunday uniform served coffee and folded out the card table, according to the tradition of the house, in the sealskin carpeted warm living room. According to Else's father, Pastor Holm from Seal Point, this little card playing tradition was an example of grievous moral depravity. As winter dragged to a close, Else disagreed, declaring it to be a great source of good-natured enjoyment to be Godfather's partner and the opponent of the local Pastor, while Godmother watched on, setting the table for evening supper. One of her favorite domestic scenes were the rigorous discussions held by her Godparents about new things beyond her normal horizon which served to stretch her young imagination into unknown territory. Her own natural curiosity craved knowledge which she hoped to acquire, and she was frustrated when Godfather ended a particular despute by reaching for a song book to sing tunes like "Cambambui" or "The Grapes do Grow." To make matters worse, he wouldn't even let her accompany him on the piano, "No, these are all to be sung a cappella," he would say, asking just for the first note from the Pastor, which got him started with the greatest enthusiasm.

"Godfather is still the same jolly fellow that gave me and Elserak raisins and dried fruit in the store on the pier at Seal Point when we were little," she wrote to her mother.

Rasmussen from Seal Point was one of those unusual characters that could be found everywhere. These fellows often came out from the Danish trades and find a master to work for who tolerates their special habits and "differences." Here at Foxhole land the local "character" was Olsen. Olsen married a Greenlandic woman and together they had a house and grown children. After he retired, Olsen had started sitting with the lads in the Sailors' Home, where hammocks were strung for sleeping watches. He stopped going home to his old wife all together, even though they had not suffered anything like a falling out. He liked her well enough, but, as he put it, "the devil no longer cared for their black kettle," an archaic expression which was supposed to serve as an explanation for his natural inclination to sleep elsewhere.

The Blacksmith from the Point and Olsen stuck to the edges of social life, since they were both Danish, both lived at the Sailors' Home,

The Two Elses

both wore sealskin pants and Fair Isle sweaters, and both considered it an immense honor to be invited to the local awards banquets. Their differences were evident in the attire they adorned themselves with at said banquets. Whereas Olsen never got dressed up, Rasmussen went with his friend "Tippo," or Deborah, who was also his caregiver. Rasmussen always had on his best, and the suit he found for these occasions came from a certain blue painted chest and though it resembled a costume of some sort, his attempt was deeply touching and admirable, for it seemed that deep down, the blacksmith was secretly something of a dandy! At least Else thought so.

Rasmussen always addressed her formally as if she were royalty or a fine lady, using the old fashioned and very formal "thou's" and "thee's" whereas Olsen just treated her like a normal mortal. She did not enjoy Olsen's lackluster performance in the manners department and she made no secret of that fact. She was not clever enough to avoid a reprimand from her Godfather when her behavior became so noticeable it was embarrassing. One night when all the guests had departed, Godfather took her aside and demanded to know why she would not offer her hand to Olsen thanking him for the goose that the Greenlander had taken down for the feast dinner. And why she had turned her head away and walked off, her back to him when they were saying goodbye? What was the reason for this rudeness? All Else could do was cry. She did not know what to say. She had not learned how to defend herself. Godmother had followed her inside and was monitoring the conversation. Deep inside she felt great relief at this sign of Else's discerning sense of propriety, which she felt just might serve as an anchor during the next phase of her education in social etiquette.

"What was Pastor Holm thinking when he wrote that Else needed to develop her sincerity and compassion for others?" she thought to herself. No, this episode was certainly proof of her inner compass, and this new dawning sense of maturity growing within Else gave Mrs. Buck new hope. At the same time, Else was, in her own way preparing a little surprise for the Bucks.

Else had not been the only passenger of importance onboard the ship Haien.

The Blacksmith's son Rasmus had finished his training in the trades had become a fine carpenter. The Inspector had posted him to Foxhole Land where his services were needed. Ramos was still not married, and his parents and many younger siblings moved out there with him to the "new country," as they called it. His family cobbled a small cottage together from abandoned walls left behind by past emigrants. They quickly assimilated into their new surroundings and were widely accepted as part of the community. Their neighbors, who were easy going when it came to house building, noted

The Two Elses

his house was no ordinary pile of blocks, compared to what Bucks called typical "seacoast hotel style"—immigrant architecture or cobbled cottages and huts known as *sajasut*.

Else's thoughts flew to these humble walls every evening. When she laid her curly head down on the snowy-white pillows, her thoughts wandered off towards a certain young carpenter with his interesting blond curly beard and his rosy cheeks. He did look so dashing in his striped wool sweater and those bright red leather suspenders crossed at the back. And didn't he look wonderfully fine, standing there with his axe chopping wood! Oh, to be a Greenlander! She would rise early and comb her hair, putting in the blue ribbon, a traditional blue ribbon worn by Greenlandic wives. She imagined how wonderful it would be to welcome home her "man" to a clean cottage neatly swept and scrubbed down, everything in its place of domestic bliss, a kitchen where hunger never dared to knock. But he did not know his way round a kayak paddle . . . never mind . . . they could keep fishing boats and fish for cod and flounder and move supplies and guide tours along the sea coast during the summer, and he could work as a carpenter. When the season for *Kabliau* came, the cliffs behind their house would be filled with the sight of drying cut fish—how wonderful it would be! But there was one thing—what would her parents say? Sleep overcame her at this point. She did not even think about what Godmother Bucks would have to say.

Godmother Bucks was quick to learn of the new developments and dealt with the "mischief" effectively. Like all good mothers and godmothers, she threw herself between Else and her "mischief," which may not have been the wisest thing she could do. Godmother Bucks navigated these tricky waters according to her own sense of political power, launching an effective campaign of disdainful remarks that hit their intended target: the black sheep of the family. This approach backfired entirely, fanning the flames of Else's first crush even more passionately. She would need an entirely different kind of medicine to change the focus of her attentions, and a solution quickly appeared. One beautiful evening she had stepped outside hoping to catch a glimpse of her beloved carpenter who had the habit of taking an evening stroll over to old Olsen the retired villager at the Seaman's home. He always passed the Magistrate's house on his way over to see Olsen, and as destiny would have it she ran into him. Without thinking, Else let loose a very deep sigh of appreciation—for as he stepped near, as any Greenlandic girl would naturally do. Without so much as a second's hesitation, without even taking his pipe out of his mouth, he said in Greenlandic, between his teeth, close enough to touch her clothes, "What

The Two Elses

on earth is wrong with you, Else?"[19]

She studied him for a long time after that. Now he seemed a bit too simple minded, he was rather plump, and those silly red crossed suspenders did look rather odd on top of his striped sweater . . . Oh Else, Else, what were you thinking? She tried to brush away the thoughts again, with laughter, but at night before falling asleep they tumbled in upon her emptiness, and she felt it like an illness creeping over her.

However, she did quickly recover from all of this drama, and Godmother Bucks silently awarded herself the victory for her clever interference.

As Else's daily life fell into a pattern, she did not have much extra time to socialize with the local Greenlanders, and that particular little episode distanced her from them even more. This was not at first a great source of dismay for her, but she suffered pangs of regret at the loss of those friendships which had sustained her over the years. Her old love for nature, her need for fresh air and the tranquility of the outdoors was resurrected on summer trips when the Bucks travelled or during nesting season when they went out in kayaks, filling them with thousands of large green eiderdown birds.

Then she enjoyed the company of the Greenlanders: she sang, told jokes, shouted out across the seas making echoes, acted out silly skits and ballads. She walked, talked and even stood like a Greenlander. She thought about Elserak without sentimentality; but those times grew far and few between as she grew more and more busy with other things. The demands of her lessons took more and more time. and socially she had many new friends from the pages of books in the Bucks library.

It was during the dinner hour at noon while the elders were enjoying their time together that Else could cultivate her love of leisurely reading. There were knighted lords and gowned ladies in pearled hats who brought along their young girls suffering from unrequited love— Else especially liked those who went mad over romance—how fascinating! "That must be the purest form of love!" she thought.

She often imagined herself to be the slighted heroine. She allowed her heart to rise and fall in the waves of sentimentality of romantic novels. She even suggested mythic names from her favorite heroines, such as Kunnigunda Sakuntala for the christening of Assistant Moe's new baby. Moe had married to the "Doctor's Kisten" and had moved to their region from Seal Point. However, Else knew her audience well and was careful not to share these interests in her letters to her mother. Instead she peppered her obser-

---

19. *"Else, sulelk atit?"*

The Two Elses

vations with wise words of wisdom which she knew her mother would appreciate, such as, "It is far more satisfying to give than to receive."

Pastor Holm on the other hand, grew more and more worried about his daughter as he searched her letters for mention of her old "Amazonian ways," as he called the free-spirit who loved everything Greenlandic, natural and outdoors. Did he send her away so she could grow tense, anxious and serious? But his wife found a way to put his heart at ease. She understood this was simply the adolescent phase of searing romance and sentimentality which would soon pass.

Mrs. Moe, who was a quiet and humble Greenlandic woman, was a great help when it came to the business of bringing Else down to earth, since she could bridge the two cultures of Else's Danish household with the native community. It was relatively easy to "talk" to Madam Moe, since she came from Seal Point and they shared many delightful conversations, having so much in common. Gradually she became more comfortable talking to all the other Greenlanders again, thank goodness, as the tension of her strained relationship to the native community had caused her great sadness. When the time came to prepare the *Amaut* for Madam's new baby, Else provided hours of artistic direction for the color patterns in the fringe and borders for the Christening blanket.

✦

Three years passed, during which time Else wrote faithfully in her Winter Sunday journals, filling up all the pages of her book. During the summer she sent her letters away and received news regularly. It wasn't until the spring of the year of her return to Seal Point, after three years of being away, that she received the following heartbreaking news. Daniel the Cook had died. How many times had her mother told her the story of Daniel the Cook standing at the foot of her bed, helping the new mother learn how to hold the new baby Else? She knew how tenderly he had watched over her, day in and day out as she grew up, as if she was his own flesh and blood daughter, Elserak's sister! And now to never see him again! There would be little joy in the summer boat ride home with this news weighing down upon her heart. She wondered why Elserak's letter breaking the news seemed short when it came to the subject of her father's passing.

Let us hear the letter!

The Two Elses

Dear Else Holm,

I have so much to tell you this time.[20] The Point is fantastically fun these days, you should try to get here as soon as you can. A month ago Captain Hans was docked in port with his ship. He has blue eyes set in a tanned face, curly blonde hair, and wears a blue suit on Sundays. I hide behind the rescue station every time he docked with the big ship, but he always went looking for me and found my hideout. I always ran away behind the dry goods ferry . . . but finally on Sunday we danced together at the barrel wharf and he said I should wait for him until next summer and we will get married and I will have Danish outfits, and I said yes! You have probably already heard father is dead and mother is very sad, but it won't be long before brother Lars will be a proper hunter; he has already taken many seal pups with his rifle, only two with harpoon and club, and now I help Sorensen's cook with rinsing and cleaning birds when they are busy and I bring mother the food I get when I am there. Igasok (the Cook) is starting to get old and your mother has been kind to me.

If only you could come back when the Danes go out on their summer hike to the mountains. It will probably be June 8th. But it is true, I almost forgot to tell you I had to be carried down the mountain from our reindeer hunt at Igdlunguak because my boots were so worn out the skin on my feet was peeling off—Epha carried me down more than two miles. He said he could because I was not very heavy and last Thursday in the Colony he asked me to marry him and I just laughed and told him he could wait until the foxes turned white.[21]

To prove that Elserak was not that coldhearted as she appears in this letter, we will look at the big picture in the drama of her life. Her mother had, especially since she was now a widow, scolded Else for refusing to eat the nourishing stews at Igdlunguak more often than she scolded her for refusing her suitor's proposal of marriage. Elserak would, on these occasions run out of the house with bright red cheeks of embarrassment. Didn't she know what best for her? And who was best for her? Yes she did, and she did not lose heart when her Captain, after their very interesting visits that summer, failed to appear the following summer, as he had indicated, as he had actually promised he would. But was it really his fault he did not come? Did he have any control over which ship he steered or which Colony he was sent to? He was docking in a different Colony this year, but did that matter? He had written to her and even sent her a shiny bright red ribbon which she put on straight away! But a year passed ... another ship came in ... and then what? She had sent messages and greetings ... but it sounded like he had married his cousin in Copenhagen!

20. *Okausiss'aka amerdlagaalluakat.*
21. *Tulugkat k'ak'ortipata, is an expression often used.*

The Two Elses

What Elserak felt about that is unknown, but she did not cry or faint upon hearing the news. Instead, she asked Fru Holm, as Pastor Holm was making preparations for his spring trip to camp at Igdlunguak, if it wouldn't be a better idea for her to accompany him, to keep his vestments in order. Else would be able to keep track of the liturgical cloths far better than his hired man, and she could paddle as well, thereby saving him the cost of one hired paddler.

When Fru Holm met Fru Sorensen that afternoon on the Colony road she couldn't speak highly enough of her qualifications, since few knew Else as well as she did, no one was more selfless and willing to serve than Elserak, specially given her strong ties to the Igdlunguak camp . . . Fru Holm also had some idea about the refusal of Cousin Epha's marriage proposal. Fru Sorensen had been harboring a less positive opinion of Elserak, ever since she had laughed at Fru Sorensen's attempt to speak Greenlandic when ordering at the store. She was relieved to have an excuse to change her low opinion about the girl, who might just be a diamond in the rough. So, Fru Sorensen's agreeable and profuse nodding, a rare sight from her, seemed to indicate that a new day had dawned in her mind and better days were ahead for the "selfless servant" Elserak.

The Pastor left for his trip and Else was with

him. She pulled earnestly at the oars and seemed to be decidedly the most cheerful of the whole company. But after a mile at sea, one of the boatmen asked to go ashore to fill the copper kettle with drinking water. At that moment Elserak jumped out of the boat with a bundle of clothes under her arm (which she secretly had ready) and, before the boatsman came back, she had changed her clothes from, head to crown, and was transformed. With lightning speed she jumped back into the boat to her place by the oars at the back of the boat. She sat there looking triumphant as she dipped her hands into the water before she took hold of the oars. Everything about her spoke volumes—about the impact which her arrival would make when she landed at her beloved Idunguak—about a legend of luck in the making, a legend of her grand arrival. She was quite a sight for sore eyes; rosy cheeks, gleaming black hair, broad bands of white with small checks of red and yellow running down the shiny coal black leggings edged in woolen ribbons of baby blue. Her leggings continued in a striking pattern of crimson running down the knees, contrasting with the fleshy shade of her boots. Her headband streaming out in the wind like a brave banner or flag—it was indeed the very ribbon her Captain had sent her—and strangely enough, it was the very first thing Cousin Epha noticed as the Pastor's boat turned into the fjord at Igdlunguak. He knew

The Two Elses

that ribbon so well—he had noticed it every time he had gone down to the Colony—it had always felt like a stab in the back to him. Else had no idea that he would feel that way about her decorative attire, which had only practical meaning for her, to tie her hair down in the wind. It had just become a habit to wear when a festive occasion called for something special.

On the other hand she had no way of knowing why Epha came running down to the beach before anyone else got there, why he was the first. She was so self-absorbed, taking charge and excitedly directing orders to him at the moment of landing that she did not stop to consider the fact that perhaps Epha was there for her, but because that was his job. "Now don't separate his waterproof boots from their felt slippers, Epha, because I am going to work on his skillinger tonight,"[22] she was saying. "Oh wait, that little suitcase has the pastor's vestments. Epha you take that one and be careful, you know how important that is and you are the best one to take it safely up to the house . . ." He obeyed but as soon as everything was unloaded and stowed away in the guest room which Amailie had declared as the designated room for the Pastor's visits, Epha paddled away in his kayak. He had no idea that Else's special gift from the Captain now meant nothing to her, nor did he know that Captain Hans had married his cousin in Copenhagen—he did not even know that the

Captain had a cousin in the first place! So Epha left to find bird nests in the western isles.

Elserak forgot all about sewing the pastor's slippers that evening. Instead, she climbed up the trail to the high mountain meadows where she had the best view over the fjord. Down below she could see, when she looked long and hard, the kayak paddling away around the last point, no bigger than a pin prick. Then she pulled her fists up to her eyes and wept bitterly for a long time. Epha, oh Epha, that dashing hunter! How she wished she had not been so quick to think the "grass was greener on the other side" . . . than her own! Now he was sailing to the western isles where only the lucky eiderdown birds would have him for a visit, and now he was fleeing from her!

Epha did indeed cut a striking figure out on the waves as he rowed himself backwards, gathering all his strength and agility with his strong arm in deft control of his paddle and boat, turning, twisting, shooting his arrow forward from the wooden bow, then bending easily and gracefully forward to retrieve it from the water. So he plied his time for a few hours hunting eider down birds in the mouth of the fjord. For a moment, he laid his paddle down and rested his

---

22. *Skillinger—she was going to sew new soles on his felt inserts.*

The Two Elses

elbows as his boat gently bobbed up and down with the waves, viewing the scene before him. It was like a painted landscape—on the left, the Colony with its many temptations, and to his right, the low Northlands and Kangek!

Should he stop and visit the folks at Nepiset Sound? No, onwards, press forwards! The evening sun was dipping low like an open fan of gold behind the Cook Islands, now doubly dark in the shadowy contrast of flaming golds and red sunset colors. That was where he wanted to go and hunt. He expected to be back for the evening mass the day after tomorrow. He did not want to let down the Pastor, who depended upon him to assist at the service. But things did not turn out according to his plans. An unexpected pod of minke whales pushed him further north, along with a good number of other harbor seal hunters, and by the time he returned back to Igdlunguak the Pastor had already left.

Fru Holm was a bit surprised to see the beautiful Elserak looking sad and miserable as she came in from her walk up to the highlands, since nothing had happened to the Pastor.

At the whaling hunt parties up north Epha heard talk of the Captains' trip to Copenhagen to marry his cousin. Epha returned to Seal Point and was dropping by with some gull eggs for Fru Sorensen . . . before the sun had set behind the Cook Islands he was knocking on "Little

Else's" door—Elserak—who opened up with a smile that was warm and welcoming despite the fact that the foxes were not showing any sign of changing color ...

✦

Else Holm did not arrive home by the date Elserak had mentioned—the date of the Danes annual backpacking trek to "Iisblinken."[23] The ice there was almost sacred, and considered to be the beautiful, white "mother lode," a source for the essence of Greenlandic culture.[24] It took considerable persuasion, even strenuous arguments and prayers to convince Magistrate Sorensen that the important affairs of state could, for the span of a week's time, easily and responsibly be taken up by his deputy, thus allowing him to accompany them on their glorious trek. Fru Sorensen had held her ground. There was no wavering, she longed to see the sights—and it was an easy victory—for the first time in 25

---

23. *Isblink is the name used by sailors as well as dwellers of the interior of Greenland, referring to the icy glaciers which seem to "blink" or sparkle in the reflection of the sun's rays.*
24. *Lap of motherhood.*

The Two Elses

years she locked her own door. She had no idea that something might happen on this great adventure while she was away—it was the kind of trip that could be called a victory lap, since her husband had promised her a silver wedding anniversary trip to Venice. She made a point of reminding him, with a certain bitter sharpness in her tone, as he lay so comfortably down in the boat rubbing his hands together, so warm and cozy in the soft down sleeping bags. But the Governor insisted that "he had plenty of Venice right here where he was, and did not need any more," as their boat glided past the blubber rendering plant warehouses on the quay. One joke followed another, and he was asked to throw down the harpoon, a sign that was to prove his power by land and by sea, since the Magistrate was not without considerable power on land, here was his chance to prove it by sea.

As the Governor leaned back comfortably in the boat enjoying the sea and the views, it was clear that he was just as powerful by land as he was by sea (on land the Colonial Magistrate had considerable power). Perhaps he would even be able to tempt the frightening Sea Nymph *Arnakuarsak* who ruled over all the creatures of the ocean to release a few of her harbor seals to make the upcoming hunting season especially plentiful.

As they enjoyed their interesting little "walkabout" adventures away from home at sea, their goal was to paddle towards the distant fjords of inland ice. They passed some of the most verdant landscapes in the land, and on the last leg of their return journey a half mile from the Colony, their yellow skin boats could be seen bobbing up and down in the waves, surrounded by a half dozen kayaks—a few of these had followed them from the inland fjords and a few were sailing out from the Colony to welcome them home. Epha had joined them at Iglunguak and was pulled up beside by the Pastor's wifes boat, where Elserak was seated as a paddler. The cheerful sounds of greetings and gossip went back and forth from the boats to the kayaks, and the greatest piece of news that was shared among the boatmen consisted of a sighting of a great ship passing the Colony—an "Englishman." They speculated and guessed until a firm belief established that the ship was looking for "the end of the world," otherwise known as the North Pole. It had quickly departed from their waters, which was a great relief for Epha, who thought he understood most of the English words that carried the news.

"Foreigners in our land!" grumbled Sorensen down into his beard. A kayak man floated right up to their boat and pulled something very important looking out of his sealskin coat with great care.

It was indeed something of great import, and he handed it over with some ceremony to Fru Sorensen.

The Two Elses

"A calling card? Frederick?" Then she gasped as she read the last name. "What is it?" exclaimed Father Sorensen. "Did he just stop by and leave his calling card?"

Indeed, as ridiculous as it may seem, that is exactly what our old friend Frederick Sorensen did. Now he was known as Frederick Jenkins on board the above mentioned ship, and he had sailed by so close to his homeland that he could drop his calling card overboard into one of the kayaks paddling close to the waterline.

Frederick had asked that his card be delivered to his *anana*, the old Greenlandic word for mother and the only word he still remembered.

✦

At about the same time Godfather was stretched out for his midday "time of self-reflection" nap in the outback country of "Foxhole Land." Godmother closed her eyes in the rocking chair and Else sat with her elbow on the window sill, playing idly with the curls of her hair. Occasionally her gaze wandered out across the harbor to the fjord and the sunny "Pastoral Meadows" and its neighboring "Zoological Gardens." This was a favored warm spot to visit, tucked away between groves of birch and willow especially during the time of great shipping traffic from Denmark. In the warm tranquility of that summer afternoon Else Holm felt a deep sense of peace greater than any other she had known, accompanied by the sudden realization that her entire life lay before her, ready to take hold of.

A little girl arrived with a small bouquet of red flowers, which she was willing to trade Godmother, for "sweets." Godmother could never refuse one of the local children, especially if they were clean. However, Else made gestures indicating that everyone was having their afternoon naps and were not to be disturbed. Else was in fact, preoccupied, leafing through her diary, which lay open, perched precariously on the narrow window sill. Her right hand attempted to keep the book open to those pages which had drawn her eye. She had discovered two themes so far.

February 4th: Yesterday Lars Enok and the Catechist Mekias went out hunting and the sun came through the living room for the first time since November. It was out for ten minutes before it sank down below the Barrel Makers Hill.

February 6th: Today Jonas Kleist and Adam Olsen went hunting and the sun is in the living room every day now.

The Two Elses

Here was a piece of fresh news—the Doctor Kisten, who was engaged to Moe the Assistant had put away her Danish wardrobe and was now only wearing Greenlandic dress which, the writer declared, suited her far better and was "much more attractive." A shadow flicked past the window and her old friend, the young carpenter, walked past and nodded to her. He was married to the Pastor's servant, the clean and beautiful Ingeborg, who moved into the so-called "Hotel" which Godfather hoped would improve under the hand of her new mistress.

It was almost time for everyone to be waking up from their afternoon naps. Suddenly, the piercing cry of "Ship Ship! *Umiarsui-it!*" shattered the peaceful silence with joy-filled peals. Godfather scrambled up from the sofa and ran out of the living room wearing only his soft seal-leather leggings, and Godmother's cap was askew as she tumbled out the door. Seeing her mother thus, Else unconsciously threw her hands up to adjust the hat that wasn't there, then quickly checked herself in the mirror as she followed her family out to sea. The cook came in out of breath from running and asked if it wasn't time to light the cannon since the harbor was blanketed in smoke so thick from the steamer you couldn't even see across the fjord to the pastoral fields. Godfather ran in to change into his proper breeches—made from either the leather of the Greenlandic *klapmyds*[25] or "motley," which were considered the most elegant choice.

He had to put on the "motleys" because he would be going onboard to do the official ceremonial welcoming honors as representative of their little settlement. Godmother ran to her pantry to check the food stores for what they would be offering the English for tea when they landed. Else ran to her room and threw on a dazzling new dress which did not flatter her as well as her regular "short waisted" dress. She was almost beside herself with excitement and anticipation over what would "come" from the ship, as she wrote a few days later in her diary, as we can read . . .

"First you must know I was speechless from the shock . . . can you believe it? We didn't even recognize each other at first," she continued without the slightest semblance of order in her writing, but he remembered everything from our trip. He said, from the time when Elserak had to jump into the brook to rescue Sorensen to the taste of Sorensen's pot roast! "And before he left he gave me a copy of Tennyson which he said was more popular in America than Uncle

---

25. *Danish gentlemen's trousers.*

The Two Elses

Tom, and in the three days that the ship Polar Bear lay for anchor we were together from morning to night which godmother said was perfectly natural—of course you would agree—oh no, of course there is naturally no question about that, we are talking about Frederick, or about the smoke that filled the harbor on Saturday from the same English ship that had set anchor down south where they would have been taking on fresh water just as they were doing here. Nobody would deny them fair winds or good seas, or water or cargo for that matter, but we had the honor—poor Frederick who had come so close to his parents without getting a chance to see them"—and so on, the endless chatter of her pen pushed on tirelessly.

The annual photographs sent so dutifully by the young Jenkins kept the Colony up to date with changes in his appearance and everyone agreed that his most recent ones indicated that he had become quite the handsome man indeed.

Preparations for the expedition continued as he stayed over in London. His sponsors had given him the name Frederick Jenkins, and he soon became unfettered by such mundane worries as pocket money. He was not able to turn down the tempting position of Doctor on call when an officer friend had recommended him. He really had joined the expedition in the hope of returning to Greenland to see his parents and if he was lucky enough, to make a trek to the

North Pole. Else had to see her friend turn his back to her a second time from the coastline of their shared homeland.

It was no wonder why the beautiful young girl with intimate knowledge of Greenland's interior could cast her magical spell over the young arctic explorer from the first day as he hung on her every word, scribbling them into his elegant leather notebook. Soon he abandoned all pretense of writing down her observations and just concentrated on the way her lips moved when she talked. By the third day he traded his notebook for Tennyson showing her his favorite passages which he asked her to read when he was "away," a task which gave her no trepidation whatsoever. Additionally, he was truly looking forward to seeing her parents again, with the old crowd at Seal Point, with his parents of course, who also shared the sorrow of their long separation. She felt she had made an impression upon him and it was returned with a deep sense of relief and gratitude.

Her return south was slow and everyone at Seal Point had to practice the art of patience.

How they all longed to see her!

But the old and tired ship "Haien" struggled when she headed into every southwest wind and when she was only six miles north of the Colony she had to lay to anchor for eight long days sheltered in a small bay. They had nothing to do to pass the time except eat, drink and

The Two Elses

sleep, drying their wet clothes when a southwest cloudburst drenched them, reading, playing chess, and going for walks inland. The hill tops around their cove offered splendid views of the horizon and their destination, where Godfather looked to deliver his "little girl back home."

There were fragrant potted plants in Else's bedroom window, which faced the grey highland meadows. The new piano-forte was a big surprise, due to the sale of Godfather's latest whale catch—he had secretly ordered the piano from Hornug & Møller to be shipped directly to the house at Seal Point.

It was wonderful to be back home again!

She had to smell the roses, pluck the keys on the piano, and gaze out at the mountains and peaks and sky. She played with her red paper viewer that showed the fairy tales of Hans Christian Andersen, so cleverly constructed by the doctor's wife as a going away present at Christmas time before her big journey to the interior.

But her reunion with Elserak was another matter—stiff, awkward, and quite cool. A wall of icy reserve sprang up between them —probably the same pattern felt by others in the story of Danish and Greenlandic friends growing apart, when one person suddenly stops and the other continues on in their development, some sense of loss is inevitable. Else felt the pain of this lost friendship a second time, while Elserak in her natural child-like innocence ran through the Greenlandic cottages telling everyone that Else Holm had changed and become "crazy" and unpredictable. The Greenlandic girl was simply baffled by Else Holm's ridiculous tearful outbursts when her mother had laughed at the sight of her childish dress, which did not fit the voluptuous curves of her now womanly figure. When Else's mother opened her arms to comfort her, Else then began to laugh, which also seemed unreasonable. No, there was definitely something "wrong" with the girl, she decided.

Later when Fru Holm had taken Elserak into the house as a domestic, their daily contact began to soften the initial awkwardness. They gradually became more open with each other and finally the iron gates that had imprisoned their respective souls swung open. They were able to sing the old songs once again and share their innermost secrets despite their differences in race and family backgrounds, respectful of the vastly contrasting roles they played in their respective cultures. Elserak was sometimes jealous, as she had been in the past, when it came to the Saturday parties hosted by Godmother, but now she wasn't envious over the parties, but irritated by the fact that Else Holm always had her nose in a book—Tennyson, as she put it, "that boring book that took her away." Before, it was Else Holm who sang so joyfully along with the smith, and now it was Elserak who chimed in to

The Two Elses

the lusty verses, which had grown in popularity with the local Greenlanders, while Else Holm buried herself in thoughts of Tennyson.

Else blushed as she read her poetry anthology, even when she was quite alone, and especially when she discovered a silken ribbon marking a special passage she had not noticed it before, nor noticed that it might conceal some hidden meaning, so she never moved it. But as she came to it, she wondered if it was a coincidence that it had lines marked which read of such interesting thoughts:

> *In the spring a young man's fancy*
> *Lightly turns to thoughts of love*

But the "Polar Bear" would be sailing for two entire years and most of a third as well!

Two springs passed since her return from the outback and still no word from the expedition up North!! Not even a garbled message from one of the itinerant seal hunters in kayaks coming down from the North—even that would have been far better than this silence. Could he be dead? "Ya, maybe," said Elserak practically.

But Frederic was alive and had many fine experiences common for a polar explorer in Melville at Baffin Bay. He was stuck in the pack ice but escaped, he anchored at a glacier which then calved, and he was tossed in circles by a water spout. He saw the moon light above Beechy Islands, sorrowful peaks where Franklin was buried, he drove sled dog trains, shot foxes, killed a bear, shot a pair of muskoxen, sang "Home Sweet Home" with some Brits, acted out skits at Christmas and Mardi Gras, and was showered with good luck everywhere except when it came to finding the North Pole itself.

As the" Polar Bear" worked her way out of her first winter imbedded in ice, the Captain decided it would be a good idea to visit one of the northernmost Danish colonies to pick up fresh sled dogs for next winter's land expeditions. At that point Frederick requested leave to travel south to Seal Point in the summer. Constant head winds made progress slow through northern Greenland, combined with surprisingly early autumn frost and ice. He only got as far as Fox Hole Country, the northernmost Colony in south Greenland before he had to start on his journey back.

This was a great disappointment but as the brave young optimist said, "there comes a spring after every winter" and so he began his preparations for the winter season, which began with sudden fury. This meant that he would spend hours in lessons reviewing his native tongue with the Pastor and visited Moes often. He also went hunting, played Bolt with the Greenlanders and cards with the Danes, danced with the girls, courted, visited and flirted with the ladies and was the talk of the town here, as he had

The Two Elses

been in Baffin Bay.

Springtime at Seal Point was a dangerous time for a young man who followed along the path of sentiments described by the great Poet.

This particular springtime fulfilled the Poet's decree exactly; by the time they were on their first mountain hike, their goal nothing less than "Little Malene's Overlook," which had ended on such an unexpected note due to Virginia's arrival, Frederick asked his childhood sweetheart if she would be willing to walk "the steep paths of life" with him, to which she promptly answered without hesitation, "yes."

They read the list hidden in the bottle by hikers who placed it in the stone wall so many years ago. It was just as stiff and unspoiled as it had been the day Assistant Moe had corked its bottle to keep it dry. They replaced the paper and put the bottle back where they found it. Who would be the next one to open it? Hardly anyone as happy as these two! Naturally . . . impossible! Perhaps it would never be opened again, it might sit there silently watching the mating calls of the grouse every spring as the high mountain snowpack and the icy glaciers calved, sending avalanches crashing down the hillsides loosened by the warm sunshine of May.

The new lovers did not want to part—it was so beautiful in that spot! They watched the sun set and listened to the waterfalls crashing down over the rocks pouring out from bottomless ice caverns up in the steep mountain peaks. They heard the deep rumble of roaring waters through crevasses and then gathering to pool in hollows before plunging down to the hills and valleys below.

There is nothing as enchanting as high mountain wilderness! The lonely traveler sees a world of natural riches as if covered in jewels and treasures fit for a royal banquet. Polished gleaming stones line the smooth floors of the high meadows, and the rare bunches of heather are bouquets presented to the guests of honor—along with the pure clarity and sweetness of mountain air!

It had been an "amazing day," the young couple declared upon their return to the Colony. Father Sorensen presented his proposal to apply for the position of regional doctor which would be open after Plum's retirement and everyone applauded its merits warmly.

✦

One summer day all the Greenlandic children, well off or dirt poor, were sent out to gather heather and branches, as much as each could carry, in exchange for prunes and raisins as promised by Fru Sorensen. But nobody other than Elserak could be trusted with the

The Two Elses

special task of bringing home the most beautiful branches of the dark green delicately leafed dwarf birch which was a fine substitute for the Laurels of other countries. Else Holm stood in front of her mirror trying on her bridal gown in the very room that looked out over the hillside and goat barn where she and her lover had promised each other "eternal friendship." The new vows they would make did not resemble their old promise made in the barn loft—this was a new plant—yet still, their fond memories of the past were fragrant flowers growing up around this new thing in the warmth of summertime. Those were the best days, and what luck, his old friends from Baffin Bay would arrive to celebrate the wedding with them! Frederick Jenkins and Else Holm!

And then, beside all those great friends arriving on the Colony ship, there were the dear old faces of folk he knew so well, with their many cases and steamer trunks filled with treasures for the Danes as well as the Greenlanders! Those were days of glory, rich and colorful, full of bustling life, visiting and socializing. The ladies had their hours gossip—gushing, teasing and blushing in front of the mirrors in the powder rooms, especially when it came to the subject of the handsome foreign marine officers.

The day came when the two Elses were to be married—even at this juncture in their lives their destinies were again entwined . . . and beautiful they both were to behold.

At twelve o'clock the Colony bells were rung ceremoniously to call everyone, including the ship men, to leave work, and at two o'clock the flag was raised on the crest of flag pole hill to signal the start of the wedding. The Greenlanders had gathered on both sides of the church doors and were hiding behind each other as usual to get the best view of the "Danish Procession." Only a few of the guests had taken their seats inside on the church pews. In the center of the group gathering at the doors, Elserak stood dressed in beautiful leather and furs adorned with ceremonial pearls around the neck and arms. German missionaries from a nearby Herrhuter Colony came wandering down from the mountains. The women had gone inside to the bride at the Sorensen place where the wedding banquet would be laid out. The men joined the visitors from both ships, the Mercantile and the local ferry, promenading along the central road and were expected to be arriving "any minute."

At last the wedding train is assembled; crinoline dresses, patent leather heels, outdated tails and tuxedos with long coats and tight shoulders, silk ties of every shape and size, and the ladies bearing amazingly inventive coiffures. You would be hard pressed to find a merrier bunch of wedding guests walking to church. The sun had never shined its happiness on two couples as unlike as these pairs as they knelt before the

The Two Elses

altar. It captured the hearts of everyone gathered for that delightful day.

The cannons exploded in honor of both marriages as they departed from the church, but the salvo of rifle shots that were fired were intended for the *Danish* bride.

The Magistrates cook and Rasmus the smith, who was dressed in his most authentic "formal wear," had organized a half dozen young Greenlanders to stand along the main Colony road with their rifles in salute.

The Greenlandic couple was also congratulated and celebrated by everyone as they left the church.

Epha and Elserak were invited to the wedding banquet in the Magistrate's house, where the great receiving rooms were transformed into grand ballrooms and banquets halls by the very talented Mrs. Sorensen.

The Greenlandic couple found a way to discreetly depart from the festivities, since she was eager to prepare her "blue ribbons" for her new husband.[26]

Soon they were all gathered together for the dance in the old barrel maker's workshop which had been swept out and transformed into a danceroom which was decorated for the occasion. Later in the afternoon the ship's cook and his bride were sent out to receive the honor of greeting the Danish bridal couple for their wedding dance. The "royal couple" received him graciously, everyone toasted them uproariously, and the Greenlanders were very impressed to see the Danish ladies and gentlemen decked out in all their finery—ball gowns and ship uniforms—to dance the formal wedding marches and waltzes.

When the Captain from the Polar Bear said his farewells that evening he said, as he patted the Colony Magistrate on the back, that "it had been a capital day, Governor!"

From the Steamship which lay to anchor in the harbor of the Colony, rockets, blue flares and fireworks ascended at regular intervals accompanied by congratulatory shouts of joy and celebration, all generated by the Greenlanders in the soft twilight of the summer night sky, illuminating the partygoers on shore.

Frederick and Else had separated themselves from their guests and had caught some free moments of peace at Seal Point. They were looking at a kayak setting out from the shore on the other side of the Steffan Egedes.

26. *During the marriage ceremnoy, the red ribbons are worn as a hair piece until the time comes when they are exchanged for the symbolic blue of married life.*

The Two Elses

This was where he had stood with his family in a tent during most of his years at sea as well as many other Greenlandic expeditions, every night the fires had cooked the great iron pots along the Flag Pole hills. The kayak they were looking at was just recently finished. They watched it push out past the point and into the bay. It was Elserak who followed Cousin Epha to Igdlunguak.

"**Elserak, Elserak**," shouted Else with emotion, waving her fine white handkerchief . . .

"Good Luck!"

"And Good Luck to you too! *Innouvdluarniaritse*! (Good Luck to both of you!)," Elseraks voice shouted cheerfully back as her boat slowly disappeared from sight.

The last sound that rose over the splash of the oars to reach the new Mrs. Else as she stood there on the beach was the melodious song of Gert which the rowers sang with each dip of their paddles as the boat pushed through the waves of the Fjord on the sea road to Igdlunguak.

✦

Teisten

✦

"Look, there is Hansen, my dear, blessed husband! And there are the little ones!" Stine exclaimed, half mumbling, as she sat with her knitting upon a mossy cliff, her back leaning against an old worn cannon. The cannon was the most northern weapon belonging to the Royal Danish Crown, and Hansen was the most northern servant of Her Majesty's Government stationed at Tingmissat, Greenland, the most northern outpost under the Danish flag. Tingmissat was a few kilometers north of the most northern colony in northern Greenland which officially

Teisten

made Stine Hansen northernmost lady in the Royal kingdom of Denmark, perhaps even in the entire world, as were their children.

Their daughter, "Little Stine," was dressed in rich skins and down dresses which made her just as wide as she was tall. She looked like an exact copy of her mother. The boy on the other hand looked like the perfect model for an Eskimo, except he was as pure as the snow that capped the mountains all around them, summer and winter. The snow that comes and goes had melted, giving rise to little flowers, children of the sunlight, who jostled for Stine's attention on her wedding day, putting on lavish displays of tender fragrant color. Stine had known the flower of flowers, the rose, from her trip back home to Denmark, but these flowers were worthy in their own splendid way of admiration and she was grateful for their appearance.

"I would not trade this spot for any place in the world," she declared, "for here the sun never sets." In her exuberance to match her words to feelings she forgot to add that in winter, the sun never rises. So, she hummed a few bars from the "Song of Cinderella,"

> *What are riches, what is happiness,*
> *What is beauty or delight?*
> *None of these will give you bliss*
> *Without a peaceful heart and a*
> *peaceful mind.*

Hansen arrived, "that beloved, blessed husband." "Here is daddy, children," Stine announced to the little ones. The children ran over and lowered the northernmost Danish flag on its flagpole, which made them proud as it was a special day.

The little house was tarred jet black, with broad white trim around its small, clean windows reflecting back the hot summer sun and guarding against noisy invasions from large Greenlandic flies eager to devour the delicate houseplants inside. Hansen had conscientiously raised and lowered the Danish flag for many national, state and religious holidays as well as for occasions warranted by his own discretionary judgment. Today the flag flew to mark the day of his wedding, it was the seventh at this outpost! The first one had been in the Royal Guard's Yard in Vesterbrogade. Stine was the daughter of a gentleman farmer from Vemmelov promised to a crofter's boy who was insanely jealous of her state. Finally she broke it off with him and took off for a boarding house in Copenhagen where she met a man named Hansen, a proper craftsman barrel maker later to be promoted to foreign service in His Majesty's Royal Company.

Although he was several years older than Stine, he offered her his heart on the condition that she would share his cottage with him at 73 degrees latitude north of the equator. She may have been naive and overly enthusiastic at the notion, but stuck to it through the years without any regrets.

The children brought in the great rolled up flag and Hansen's work for the day was concluded, as far as he knew. He sat down to enjoy the sight of his lovely ham dinner being prepared.

"I hope Metes is watching the fire!" shouted Stine, which summed up the practical thoughts of her husband exactly at that moment. The response to this hope arrived as a cloud of exuberant blue smoke burst from the cooking fire which was supposed to be cooking the ham.

"William is taking a long nap," Hansen said as he settled in. "He is positively sweating bricks from the sheer effort of his snoring!"

Stine threw down her knitting and ran in to make sure that Metes the nanny, in her eagerness to attend to the smoking ham, did not accidentally smother the baby in her cradle. But all was well—"nobody overboard" as Stine put it—and she sat down again. However, her knitting was now tangled around Little Stine's legs and around the Little Eskimo's rather stout legs since both were tumbling upside down on top of Hansen who had collapsed on the sofa.

A Greenlandic woman walked by between the grassy thatched cottages.

"You know that there is going to be a wedding party tonight at Times," Hansen said. Stine answered that she did not think it was really a "wedding" and that people shouldn't get married without a marriage ceremony first. Hansen took up the cause of the underdog (or "devils," as he truly put it). "What else should they do?" he blustered, "when, if they are lucky they have a dozen miles to walk for a priest, and in the worst case they can't get one at all? And it was none of her business to judge anyway," she admitted.

"No, you are right about that," Hansen answered, "since you are so privileged it is not quite fair to condemn others."

"I know about these matters from first hand experience, I might add."

Stine quickly looked up from her knitting as he continued. "Since I am such a dashingly handsome fellow myself," he continued unabashed, stroking his chin whiskers with relish, and since I was once slightly engaged . . . and I am not alone in that respect . . ."

At this point Stine's face darkened considerably but Hansen powered on, continuing the tale. If it had not been for the long journey to reach the minister in those days Stine would have never reached the North Pole, since a certain Dort would have made the nicest little woman to warm his blankets . . .

"Say friend," interrupted Stine vehemently.

"However, I was determined, oddly enough, to be married with a minister and a proper wedding ceremony, no two ways about it. He ended his story by drawing his finger across his throat to indicate his willingness to give his head as proof of his obedient promise to Stine should she require it. In any case, Dort was already happily married to her Greenlander Savernek and would have not been any happier had she stayed with Hansen, in his opinion.

"But what in Hell's name is that?" Hansen jumped up in alarm.

A kayak swept silently into the harbor as if powered by some hidden steam engine. Two men sprang out and ran up to Hansen's place. "You have to come with us, right away, *Pitak*." (*Pitak* was the term of endearment the local Greenlanders used for Hansen, meaning kind and good.) "Barselais' wife died in childbirth and they want to bury her baby alive with her in her grave. Like the heathens used to do long ago."

"Get my hat, Stine!"

"On our wedding day?" whined Stine, rather selfishly.

"What about the ham? "

"It will keep!" shouted Hansen, one leg already in the boat.

"The whole business will only take three, maybe four hours, if we can take the back roads," he said, looking at his dedicated rescuers who nodded, positively affirming his estimate."

Stine clammed up, partly due to Hansen's

abrupt orders, and partly because of the unexpected separation on their wedding day, but even more at the thought of the motherless child at Igdlokut. As she gathered up her own little ones by the hand to go home, Stine plucked a handful of the fragrant creeping phlox growing in the shelter of a stone wall, protected from the icy winds. She sprinkled the blossoms over a tiny grave marked by a small white picket fence. She tried to shake off her melancholy as she put the children to bed and set the festive table for her husband's return. Busying herself with these little tasks helped to restore her equanimity somewhat.

At Igdlokut, Barsilai, the grief-stricken baby's father was determined to allow the newborn infant to follow her mother back to heaven, sleeping peacefully in her mothers arms, as opposed to "wakening on the harsh deathbed of the mothers' cold grave," as he put it. And of course the child would die anyway without milk, since there were no nursing mothers in their region to feed her.

"A child such as this cannot eat what we eat," he stated with finality.

Hansen was moved and thought carefully; "There is more to this than I ever realized—seal blubber? Dried fish, that tears your throat like needles? Frozen liver and ice water? He was right, an infant cannot survive on such food. But we can't just go and bury a living human being! What are you thinking *kussimangitsut*[1]?" he exclaimed sincerely, without the least Danish superiority over the Greenlander.

"No, but our sorrow is too great for this tiny motherless child," answered Barsilai with conviction.

Yes, we can all have our opinions about this tragedy, thought the foreigner, as he suggested they bundle up that little "person there."

"I'll take it with me, and Stine will nurse her with a bottle."

The father understood enough of the talk to gather that his child would be cared for, so he gave it up willingly.

"Has she been christened?"

"No."

"Send for the Catechist immediately then!"

But the catechist was out hunting.

Hansen hoped the infant would survive the trip back home. He carried her back in his arms, wrapped in a blanket made from downy feathers, mostly from the Teisten birds.

What will Stine say, he thought on his way back. She did not like the idea of his little sweetheart—that was probably just a matter of time and she would soften—she was so good and understanding, considering how hard it really was to live at these latitudes, he mumbled to himself.

"Well, lets get those paddles moving, children!"

As the sun began to fall down towards the

horizon, with a wink of an eye the same kayaks were left with their contents beached at Tingmissat. It was midnight; the dusky light was quietly glowing in the cozy living room as Hansen walked through the door with a "fitting" wedding gift for his bride.

"Wouldn't that be a better gift for Dorthe at Savernek?" Stine asked bitterly. But she instantly regretted her words. How could she so quickly forget all her vows, promises and good intentions?

As she served the ham, she considered her husband's great act of compassion with the devotion of a loving wife—few would have done as he had.

And so the wedding day ended with just as much joy as it had begun.

✦

The rescued child was happily christened, but the name she received was hardly ever used. The blanket she had been wrapped in for her first journey home gave her the name she carried for the remainder of her life. It was made from feathers of Serfak, which translates to

---

1. Heathens.

Teisten

Teisten, and that is what the little girl was called by everyone, near and far. Nobody ever used, and fewer still ever knew her christened name. Hansen took up the thread from those bitter words from Stine. Hansen regarded Dorthe's qualifications to receive the child. He realized that it would be a great burden indeed to expect his wife to raise such a helpless child.

Dorthe and her new husband were, at that moment, packed and ready to leave Savernak and travel to Tingmissat to live, so Hansen asked her to raise the child with a modest monthly stipend for her daily care.

✦

The little Serfak, (the Hansen's always called her Teisten) thrived, grew and looked like a happy little Greenlander in every way. However, her personality was quite unusual. It seemed as if a shadow from her harsh beginning hovered over her. She did not play or laugh like other children. She paid dearly for these differences; the other Greenlandic children taunted and teased her mercilessly, as children anywhere will do among themselves. Teisten was tortured and bullied in every way imaginable: they pulled her pony tail out when her foster mother had just done her hair, her perfectly sculpted nose they called a siko or beak, and she was always referred to as a *Pitak's kimissak*, "Hansen's house pet," by the other children. Birds were often tamed and kept indoors as pets for children in Greenland. All this added to Teistan's withdrawn nature. One day the biggest and meanest of the bullies greeted her with a new ditty created for her, and all the others joined in.

> *See how she hops and laughs and dances*
> *Teisten of the Feather Skins*
> *Such a great show to see how she prances*
> *And she will bow and nodd to the applause!*
> *Aggmanik, serfanik, timmialik*[2]

Teisten ran home weeping and stayed in bed by her mothers side for a very long time.
She grew more and more unhappy and wounded by their teasing until she could take it no longer. By Christmas, the season "where everyone is filled with happiness," she thought about going away to the interior, far away from people, which she knew from stories her people told from time to time. She found comfort in this idea which grew over time and one day courageously put on her fur jacket and began her flight. She reached the end of the long valley

---

2. The last line is Greenlandic for the second line in the verse.

where she had to turn her way up and away from the sight of her home and the other huts of the village. There she lost heart and gave up, realizing that, despite her sorrows, she was not quite ready to become a modern day Salik.[3] Salik had seemed to live a life of bliss, living in an igloo far away in a deep valley somewhere, one winter here, another there, just like the mountaineers ... talking to wild animals, the hares and fox kits, who were enchanted human beings to keep him company, and who were far kinder than any real human beings, who only caused pain and sadness;

> *See how she hops and laughs and dances*
> *Teisten of the Feather Skins*
> *Aggmanik, serfanik, timmialik*

Despite the bitter taste of those chants that haunted her wherever she went, she made the decision to turn around and follow the friendly curl of smoke rising from her foster mothers chimney. As she looked around she did feel a bit lost; up and down and in, toward the great and silent eastern sky, as if her legs themselves could speak. She knelt down to recite the prayer of her people when faced with great fear: *Gutiâ, saimânga ajortiliuˆgsama,* Forgive me for my sins dear God."

She could not stay in that position for long, the cold was so bitter it felt like needles, so she stood up, relieved by the prayer, and instead of continuing her journey east she turned around and began to run back home, westward bound. Sometimes she could sit down and slide down the steep, icy hills and by the time she reached her village, people were pouring into the Catechist's house (if it is even possible to say a handful of people were pouring).

✦

It was Christmas Eve! The flag had been flying from Hansen's house all day, lit by the bright moon.

The sun had been a stranger for some time, but "*Uvatsie*! Wait!," explained Mrs. Hansen to her children when her children asked why the moon was always their sun in the winter. "Just wait! Things take time! Soon enough the sun will come back and it will stay up all day and all night long and we can pick flowers by the fence and play tag by the cannon." The fence and the cannon were buried under a deep layer of snow, many yards high just then. Hansen's house looked like a white box made of snow with a

---

3. Salik was a hermit according to Greenlandic legend. Read further in Tales and Traditions of the Eskimo by H. Rink.

Teisten

long path up to the door that led to the other buildings in the village. The windows facing the main road were protected from snow drifts during snowstorms. It was Hansen and the local villagers who kept the path clear. Hansen enjoyed the exercise which helped against cabin-fever and the villagers liked to have a way to go visiting. The towering walls of snow looked like giant blocks of white marble in a castle fortress built of ice, where the children, including Hansen's, loved to storm about, dancing and playing.

This night was quiet, however, as the villagers formed a procession, led by their Catechist. As soon as Stine heard the sounds of their singing, the shutters fell down from the windows of her soul. She saw the light streaming from brass candle flames which were lit, alongside the lamps which had been on night and day the last few months, to welcome the congregation inside. Hansen's older children ran out and joined the Greenlandic children while father and mother sat with the little ones on their laps, who listened reverently as long as the service lasted. Outside the bright winter stars competed with the flaming curtains of northern lights until the early morning hours of Christmas Day.

When Serfak, or Teisten, dressed in her festive best like the other children, went to the Catechist's house on Christmas Day Service, as the stars were beginning to fade, her young heart was filled with peace. That night she had a wonderful dream; she was standing out on the ice on the playing field when she suddenly saw the beach open up to the land of the *innersuit* where her deceased mother lived. Her mother came out of a tent and waved to her but she did not move her feet quickly enough and they were stuck in the ice. Her mother saw this and looked upon her with a love and kindness as only the dead can give. Her look seemed to tell her that there was no need to feel sadness or sorrow anymore, and that from that moment she would always find happiness and joy in her heart. That dream, along with the brightness of the moonlight streaming down between the icy inland glaciers and sparkling white mountain valley floors was such a blessing. But in the land of *innersuits*[4] where the ghost had come from, summer filled the land and the mountainsides were brown, dotted with shimmering lakes. It felt so dark, so very dark to see her mother once more disappear again behind the flap of the tent as if she was no longer her mother . . . and the beach where spirits of innersuits land closed again.

4. *Long ago when people lived by the rule of superstition, Innersuit land was an imaginary place where eternal summer tempd human beings to cross the threshold between the living and the spirit world. People paddled in kayaks and ate seal meat, everyone was good and invisible guardian spirits protected kayak men from drowning.*

Teisten

✦

But the years flew by, and with their passing, which seemed so swift, Old Stine never felt quite finished, especially in the winters. She had more than enough on her plate with all the duties of a housewife keeping track of Hansen, his children, his china, starching the linens, polishing the copperware, everything held to the highest standards of domestic order. Over time she commanded great authority in local matters and even had to travel by sled to the neighboring village, Igdlokut, to help out when they needed her. She tried to avoid making a habit of this, since things at home usually suffered in her absence; once Hansen burned a hole in the floor when he dropped burning coals and he even used one of the fine linens to lift the blackest of pots off the stove.

Teisten grew up and matured, but her quiet, introverted nature never left her. She left behind the fears and anxiety of those early years, but her nature remained thoughtful and introspective. Outwardly, she lived in close connection with nature, which opened her to the world of Greenlandic sagas through her Greenlandic foster father. She loved the northern lights, the stars and the moon with its sorrowful face, for it also had suffered greatly! Bénja had told her that the moon had been a Greenlander at first who suffered with love for sister Sun.

Bénja (short for Benjamin) was a youth in his twenties who excelled at everything. He was the strongest sled driver, and the best ball player. He had always been the kindest to Teisten, which made her feel so happy; the kind of happiness that she felt when her foster father stroked her cheeks in praise or held her by the chin in admiration.

The years passed and Hansen's children grew up with them. Both the "Little Eskimo" and "Cradle William" had been sent to Denmark. By the time she had been married for twenty four years, her daughter "Little Stine" was twenty and had married a Danish carpenter from a neighboring colony. Twenty four years! It was no wonder she had grown fond of her place in the north. Peace and joy lived within these black-tarred cottages and huts at the base of the grey mountains of Greenland!

✦

Teisten

For Teisten, Mrs. Hansen had become her one and only source of stability, comfort and happiness. She was happiest when she stayed with her in the Danish house where she had always felt protected by strong wings. Her greatest wish was to become officially part of the Hansen family and travel with them on their upcoming trip home to Denmark, which had been suggested once or twice.

It would be hard to convey the Bengalise light that painted Teisten's picture of the exotic foreign land she dreamed of travelling to- just as hard as it is to convey to the reader the indescribable raw beauty of the place where Teisten was born, with winter's aurora borealis, the light that would affect her very destiny and sweep away Mrs. Hansen's dreams of seeing Teisten dressed as a "true Dane."

One evening Tingmissat's residents were playing ball on the ice. They played a community game for both old and young, men and women. Afterwards they divided into two teams for long ball, with plenty of kicking and running. There was life on the ice that day! The children ran around the village center in and out of the fenced in circle, drawn out to the twilight edges of cavernous alleys made by glacier walls that reflected the mysterious green yellow curtains of northern lights streaming and dancing down from the far reaches of the sky like flaming swords held by invisible hands.

None of the players paid much attention to the dancing lights, as engrossed as they were with their ball, a simple sausage shaped leather thing reminiscent of *Molbo* stories from Jutland.

The black ball spun around in the hard packed snow, blasting it to showers of crystalline dust that rained down in clouds. The crowd watched with intense curiosity as the two rivals grabbed each other around the waist to get the final score that would bring down the house in shouts of glory. They gave each other a kind of death blow, shoving hip to hip and flew so far apart that in the end the ball flew away and the tie breaking point went unclaimed.

Benja arrived just at that moment, returning from a long sled dog trip. The crowd began a long, low rumble. Now something will final happen. "Our ringer has finally arrived!" somebody shouted as Benja jumped in between the dueling players and with one great thrust from his elbow split them "like schools of herring in the sea," as the Greenlandic legends would say. He pulled up and crossed his arms, giving the ball a confident kick with the inside of his foot. As the crowd roared the ball sailed over their heads and fell outside the ring. Teisten noticed for the first time that Benja held himself more upright than the others, oddly enough, and was stronger and more handsome than the other Greenlanders. But why was she even noticing

Teisten

that now? He had always been that way! Maybe it was just a trick of the magical northern lights that made him stand out like a hero the moment he came striding over the playing field to the center of the ring.

✦

One winter day eight dog sleds from Tingmissat were gathered together in the village center. They were ready for a journey to Igdlokut, a few miles over the ice followed by a mile by land.

Igdlokutfjeldet, where Teisten had first opened her eyes to the light of the sun, was a half circle of steep, black cliffs which played an important role in the question of sunlight, for this was the spot from which the sun could be seen returning after months of darkness. This too was the place where the sun disappeared after the harvest, sending its last rays of farewell to summer. This was a sacred site where the world transitioned.

Hansen had been at Tingmissat for 27 years but he had not yet been to the site of the Sunfest, or return of the sun, for this celebrated moment. Up until now they had lived quietly without ever attending one of these celebrations, but they couldn't leave Greenland without having witnessed the ceremony on the peak of Igdlokuttjeldet at least once.

The weather was extremely cold; a biting frost, calm and clear as it could be at the North Pole. They did not seem to mind, since they were all wrapped to the very tip of their noses in warm bear skins and other furs as the sled team driver cracked the whip, calling to the lead dog to behave himself and set a good example for his mates. Hansen had a good sled that ran over hill and dale effortlessly towards Igdlokut. Hansen wanted Teisten to go on Benja's empty sled travelling next to his, as opposed to the other sleds that had jumped the gun and were just ahead of them. Teisten had been too shy and would have none of it.

"Oh how the snow smells so good, mother!" shouted Hansen's eight year old Wilhelmine as she opened her mouth to taste the clear frosty air ... "And what is that bird mother?" she continued, pointing out with an arm that looked more like a leg with all its warm packaging.

"They are ravens, and they are flying in circles over Igdlokut," explained Mrs. Hansen, who added that where ravens flew, there were also people, people who made waste, and the ravens were drawn to their garbage. Seal heads, frozen entrails and leftover waste from the hunt that the greedy dogs did not eat. Ravens belonged to the top of Iglokutfjeldet, as did Teisten, according to what Hansen told his sled companions.

Teisten

They joked that, as a native Greenlander, Teisten knew enough about the native birds to not put ravens, teister, seagulls and land birds together under the same roof. With such warm-hearted banter and chatter they reached at last the small pile of snow under the high clear mountains that was Teisten's birthing place, Igdlokut.

Old Barsilai had, since the Hansen's took care of his child, become part of their family, at least in his own humble estimation. He showed this feeling of kinship in a number of different ways. Now he grabbed the reins of Hansen's dogsled and turned out the dogs for him. Everyone else stood harnessed on the south side of the mountain where many others had arrived for the festivities. The tired dogs lay down in twisted leads and piled up in bunches. For now, the work to reach their masters would truly begin for them in earnest.

There were about a hundred people, men women and children all in furs and everyone focused on getting Mrs. Hansen up to the top, an arduous task, since she was no mountaineer. The heavy winter garments did not make movement any easier for her!

She resembled a bear as she put one foot forward in the snow, with her fuzzy mittens. She was surrounded and supported on both sides and some even pushed from behind, so she was able to make it to the top. Teisten and Wilhelmine had already arrived and had been waiting for some time.

The sky was cloudless. It promised to be a clear day. A softness still lay over the landscape. Hansen grabbed his pocket and exclaimed: "Damned watch! Stopped by the cold! Nine? It was nine when we left! When it says twelve, we have it! (He meant the sun.) Good thing it didn't stop!" He continued circling his sled around for Stine. From the peak of Igdlokutfjeldet with its steep sides which overshadowed all the eastern views below on the valley floor, a new and strange world unfolded before them. A land of snow covered alps; rugged blue black ridges, saw tooth craggy tips like church spires, contrasting with gently rolling snow-covered fields. Old Barsilaie softly etched its essence when he said *arkit usornarsilè*-hallowed be thy name.

A cloud edged in rose drifted up towards the white peaks but was not strong enough to lighten the darkness of the bottomless Dalparti gulf below, forming the middle ground between the inland mountains and Igdlokut. They trampled the snow down to keep their feet warm, and to relieve their impatience, keeping their gaze fixed on the highest snowy peaks. Another streak of rose awakened their enthusiasm, followed by another, and at last a whole series of rose-gilded clouds gathered into the most fantastic tableau. Wilhelmine erupted in joy, while the practical Greenlanders forecasted easterly winds.

They counted the minutes.

Teisten

Suddenly it was there! *Â-uta*! Sounded like the beating of wings through the group watching. Another trumpet blast of royal colors—fiery red-purple light heralding the arrival of the Majesty himself. Soon afterwards the deep resonance of everyone's "*á-uta!*" rose through the crowd as the light of lights, the beautiful sun rose upwards slowly and stately until it stopped and hung above the peak—that is how it appeared when the mountain sides no longer measured its height, like an incredible opal in a garland of whispering clouds.

After a quick "hello" to the "King of Light" everyone went down to the house of Barsilais. Inside the air was not as clear as the mountain top breezes they had just enjoyed; but the change served everyone well—at least the Hansen's were grateful as they sat with their great cups of coffee to warm up. The oil lamps were lit again, since it would be two weeks until the sun came all the way around to the bottom of the valley floor. Every bed had its own lamp and each sleeper took the greatest of care with it. The moon rose late that day. The homeward journey with sled dogs would be by moonlight. A white back whale had been caught the day before and it needed to be gutted and divided among the community. There was more than an appetite for whale meat among the Greenlanders that day. There was a restless feeling of festive drunkenness. They gathered at Barsilais house to play and swap stories. Stine sat on the edge of the sofa with her feet resting on the floor while Wilhelmine sat in the darkened middle of the sleeping platform far from the edge, a spot that feels like the last rows at the back of a theater where nobody notices if you stand up to see. The entertainment was in full swing. An older Greenlander had given a talk about the rhythmic movements of blue-ice flows at high elevation—*oh Ya!*—where the male reindeer, that enormous fellow drinks from frothy streams—*oh Ya!*—those high green meadows where the female grazes with her calf—*oh Ya!*—the best places to hike in the summer—*oh ja! immâk'jâh!*

It was warm in the crowded room, very warm. Everyone did what he or she felt best to cast off some layers for comfort.

Then Bènja stood up and like a true Greenlander, tossed his long hair back to make a statement. He began to tell the story of his recent journey to K., a place known by very few of the folks in Tingmissat.

Just as the speaker before him had followed the male reindeer across the blue-veined ice, Bènja described in verse and prose how he had guided the strident lead dog of his sled team with the crack of his whip towards the far away place. The good men at K. with their huge hats could only be Amauts. The good women there had a weakness for snuff, and when they ran out of it they tried to use powdered stones that chaffed their nostrils. There were several more complaints about the people up there that followed, accompanied by resounding appreciative applause from the audience. Suddenly Bènja shifted his tone from a satirical ballad, introducing Malene, a dark horse of a spinster who had an unusual personality.

> *The way she used her tongue*
> *The way she used her tongue*
> *Malene*
> *Malene, stood out as the only one!*
> *Nobody else like her*
> *She smiled at every man*
> *Only Malene, Malene!....*

After two verses, which were sung, according the poetic custom of the time, to a familiar tune, Bènja began to clap his hands rhythmically above his head to an old-fashioned drumbeat while his feet stepped out the beat. After this inserted tale he dropped the poetic style, drew a deep breath, straightened his leather jacket and flipped his hair back behind his ears again. This signaled the coda of a long saga in traditional verse about the blue-veined ice sung only for those "gentle of soul and tender of heart" who "travel in silence" as "befits only a woman, who serves her man."

The company gave him thundering applause. When our heroic ball player and singer turned his face towards Teisten, he was so grateful that his words of icy satire had not wounded her. She was utterly happy. It was true, what her mother had told her. Her dream of the Land of the Innersuits was a signal that happiness would be hers; from that point her sadness and sorrow had become bearable—and this day she knew that they had all but faded away.

✦

The moon was up and the sleds were all ready. The Hansen's were ready . . . except Teisten was missing. After they had departed she came back. She seemed at first surprised to see they had already left without her. She had gone for a short walk up in the valley—the moon was so beautiful! How lucky that Benja's sled was still there. But what about Teisten's shyness? It had been a bad case, but now she had no choice. She sat in his sled as Bènja lashed the whip, the sled flying across the snow pushed by the eastern winds that drove hard against man and beast. They flew at great speed, but as soon as they could no longer see the settlement behind them, he jumped onto the sled. As any good doctor would, he had to gently rub a ball of snow down Teisten's very pale cheek—for she had grown as white as the snow itself. Frosty cheeks are warmed with the

Teisten

sympathetic touch of more frost, and he continued to rub until she responded with good color. But now his hands were frozen and as one good deed deserves another, Serfak offered in all innocence to warm his hands in her fur muffler which happened to be wide enough for two hands. He also knew she had on a very soft downy undergarment and perhaps he might explore that to see if Teisten's heart was pounding for him. He was quick to throw his arm around her waist as he grabbed the whip and picked up the lines after giving the dogs a break. They were now all homeward bound in a great gallop over the showering snow under a sky filled with the mysterious dancing northern lights. As they drew closer to their settlement Bènja swung back into the proper position for a driver behind the front platform. The Hansen's thanked him for bringing Teisten home safely! . . .

Teisten was so happy. Since Bènja's wordless declaration of love on that sled trip on the Sunfest Day, Teisten knew in her heart what every proper Greenlandic woman knows only too well. She had to pretend that she did not understand, or to be accurate, that she did not want to *believe* his declaration could be true. She became silent and quiet in her bearing as she went about her daily life at the Hansens.

Mrs. Hansen, who had never studied the personality of any individual Greenlander nor the Greenlandic people as a whole, was quite perplexed as to what to think about the girl. Hansen, on the other hand had more experience on the land and had made his own observations of life. He said to his wife, "when a young woman acts like that, it is because she has a sweetheart, so you better find a new housekeeper!"

"My goodness!" exclaimed Mrs. Hansen, shocked, since she must have thought that Teisten would prefer to make vows for a life of celibacy. "And right before we are to sail back to Denmark."

The debate about that question continued between the easy-going Hansen, whose nickname *Pitak* was given because of his gentleness, and his wife who, in her way, respected the Greenlanders, but who also saw them as being further from God than, for example, herself, Hansen and her children.

The unavoidable period of courtship was no easy time for Teisten; she looked forward to its conclusion with great longing. Would he visit her again? Was he interested in other girls? What would happen, would happen, and she could do nothing about it. Only Malene would do something like that.

One afternoon a messenger came to say that Serfak was invited to coffee at Bènja's house. Teisten shuddered in joy and fear at the same time. Finally the hour she had been waiting for months with deep longing for, had come. She

Teisten

was not going to let him second guess her intentions either. She wanted to leave her house at once! But it would not look right to "run," it would not be proper!

Her red, blushing cheeks slid down bashfully into her fur anorak collar.

"But Serfak! Why won't you go since you have been invited! "

"*Assukiak*! I don't know."

"No?"

"Yes. I won't be coming back here then."

"*Arime*! What did I tell you, wife," exclaimed Hansen.

"But you must go, little Serfak!"

So she folded her arms across her middle, her head tilted to one side, and she walked slowly down to the Greenlander's house.

Bènja was sitting on guard in the living room on the edge of the sleeping platform so he could watch the door. He decided he would take Serfak for better and for worse and he knew the gravity of the decision. She was well aware of the importance of this moment, that he had planned their wedding day carefully.

The house was full of people. They were drinking coffee and chatting excitedly, paying no attention to the main event about to unfold. Only Teisten sat in silence on the sofa.

Finally everyone began to go home and new guests stopped arriving. Bènja said nothing and did not leave his spot at the door. His family settled into their respective places on the sleeping platform as the girl sat unmoving with her hands over her head looking like a tragic figure deep in sorrow. Many women would sit in this way for days, either because they protested their match or because they were rejected, or because of a certain misguided belief that this tradition of exaggerated bridal modesty was a boon for the marriage. But Serfak was not pretending. When things finally quieted down Serfak slowly pulled off her tall red leather boots, set them together and resumed her hopeless position of modesty.

When everyone seemed asleep, even down to the snoring sled dogs in the breezeway, the bridegroom stood up, went over and lay down by his bride's side, sleeping through the night. The boots were a sign that the bird was ready to be caught. He did not need to stand guard at the door the next day, but instead could go hunting with a light step, whistling to himself.

Serfak went back the next day to gather her things from her foster mother's house and from Hansen's—her lamp and lamp pot, ash box, a leather bag for carrying her clothes—she had more items than many others, for Serfak was a wealthy bride and these things she took to the new place.

Bènja's old mother spread out new reindeer skins for her new daughter-in-law. When the hunter returned with his prize he found his

Teisten

bride ready for her bridegroom.

When the Hansen's left Tingmissat the following summer, old Stine insisted Serfak and Bènja accompany them to the nearby colony to have their marriage blessed in a church. She did likewise for the christening of their first born child named Hans, after Hansen.

But like his mother, this child did not end up using his christened name. Even today, as an old man he is called *Pitap atè,* or Pitax, just as Hansen himself.

✦

Biographical note

Signe Rink (née Miller, 1836–1909) was born and raised in Greenland. At age 14 she was sent to Denmark to be educated and while there she met and married geologist Johannes Rink. Through her husband's work, they returned to Greenland and began many initiatives, including the first newspaper (Atuagagdliutit, 1861–present) and in-depth studies of the Greenlandic culture (The Eskimo tribes: their distributions and characteristics, especially in regard to language, with a comparative vocabulary and a sketchmap).

Eden of The North was written after Rink returned to Denmark in 1883, and was followed by two novels, in 1886 and 1902.

She remains the first female interpreter of Greenlandic culture and maintains a poetic style only achieved by the deepest of empathies developed after many years of living and working among Inuit as a woman and as a scientist.

This is the first english translation of this work.